Betsy Ross's Five Pointed Star

Elizabeth Claypoole, Quaker Flag Maker
—A Historical Perspective

Betsy Ross's Five Pointed Star

Elizabeth Claypoole, Quaker Flag Maker
—A Historical Perspective

John B Harker (signature)

John B. Harker

with Museum Images & Exhibits

Canmore Press

Canmore Press, P.O. Box 510794 Melbourne Beach, FL 32951-0794; www.canmorepress.com

Published 2005
Printed in the United States of America, archival paper by C & R Designs, Inc., 1227 Garden Street Titusville, FL 32796; www.print123.com

Cover: Detail, *George Washington (1732-1799) at the Battle of Princeton, Jan. 3, 1777*. Princeton University. Commissioned by the trustees. Used with permission from Princeton University.

All exhibits, images, art, and graphics used with permission as described on pages 153-154.

Cover, content, and front plate design by Lyn Cope-Robinson.

This book was set in Brioso Pro typeface designed by Robert Slimbach, Adobe Systems, Inc.

Library of Congress Control Number: 2005923921
Harker, John Balderston 1922-

| ISBN 1-887774-15-7 | Paper back | US $20.00 | Canada $26.00 |
| ISBN 1-887774-19-X | Library hardcover | US $25.00 | Canada $32.00 |

Dedication

*T*his book is dedicated to the generations who have created the United States as it is today. They pass it on as their gift and challenge to future generations of "Americans" from whatever background. The hope is that this Democracy will not fail but come to be *"One Nation under God;"* truly *"of the People, for the People and by the People;"* and *"with Liberty and Justice for All."*

Acknowledgements

There are a number of people who have been instrumental in my developing the material for this book. First, Nancy Balderston Conrad, a cousin who has supplied books and family records, and helped me avoid mistakes. Another cousin, Cathy Jones Gaskill recommended my publisher/book designer to me, Lyn Cope-Robinson of Canmore Press. Cousin T. Canby Jones supplied pictures from his family files. Lastly, in the 'information provided' department are the Reference Librarians of the Falmouth (Massachusetts) Public Library. I was amazed whenever an old book would be located and brought forward through Inter-Library Loan system for my purposes.

At all times, my wife Isabella, my sons Scott and John, and my daughters Michele and Sandra have been good listeners as I brought them up to date on the latest facts, and interpretations of them with which I was working.

Two ladies of inestimable importance were Lori Dillard Rech, Executive Director of the Betsy Ross House, and Lisa Acker Moulder, the Collections Manager. "Art as Evidence" by Weston Adams was brought to my attention by them. Personal contacts with Weston Adams brought challenges regarding some of my assumptions and forced important reconsiderations of developing conclusions.

Pat Pilling, Trustee of the Star-Spangled Banner Flag House in Baltimore, edited the Appendix on Rebecca Young and also supplied previously unknown information about Elizabeth Ashburn making musket balls. (See Timeline).

Dr. Whitney Smith directed me to sources, and his paper *Face to Face with Betsy Ross* alerted me to the existence of the Samuel Waldo painting of Elizabeth Claypoole. Dr. Henry W. Moeller was kind enough to give an earlier version of my manuscript a careful reading and offer suggestions. My sister Kate and her husband, Robert Vaughan were given access to the *Pattern for Stars*, owned by the Society of Free Quakers, through the kind assistance of Karie Diethorn, Senior Curator of the Independence National Historical Park in Philadelphia.

Other sources of information, helpfully utilized, were the Historical Society of Pennsylvania, the American Philosophical Society in Philadelphia (which is the repository of the records of the Society of Free Quakers), the American Antiquarian Society in Worcester, Massachusetts, and the Huntington Library in San Marino, California which holds the Canby/Balderston papers. A researcher in Harrisburg, Pennsylvania, Alfreda P. Davidson extracted valuable information from the state library, from the thin leads I supplied.

Others who have contributed important information include JoAnn Menezes who wrote a strong feminist view of the dismissal of the Betsy Ross story by authors of flag history, and who worked with Charles Weisgerber II, grandson of the artist, in the restoration of the famous 1893 painting. The Weisgerber/Spruance family is now in its fifth generation with 110 years of dedicated work in behalf of the Betsy Ross House and the 1893 painting "Birth of Our Nation's Flag."

The bibliography was initially organized by Lucy Barron, following *Chicago Manual of Style*, and she proofread an early edition. People involved in proofing later editions at various times include cousin T. Canby Jones, my brother George, nephew Bruce Harker, North American Vexillological Association (NAVA) member Edward B. Kaye who undertook a detailed editing, and David Robinson who provided final editing assistance. And last but not least, the book design and layout was creatively visualized by Lyn Cope-Robinson, who is also responsible for the cover.

Foreword

On June 12, 1992, the *Wall Street Journal* featured article (front page, left hand column) had the headline:

Tale of Betsy Ross, It Seems, Was Made Out of Whole Cloth

* * *

A Grandson Spun a Flag Story, Then Sold It to America; Now Part of Nation's Fabric

By VALERIE REITMAN
Staff Reporter of THE WALL STREET JOURNAL
PHILADELPHIA — The story of Betsy
Ross as America's matriarch and most fa-

The grandson was William J. Canby, my grandfather's uncle, who gave a speech on Betsy Ross to the Historical Society of Pennsylvania in 1870; it was based on family "folklore" but hardly a "spun" story.

This article by staff reporter Valerie Reitman begins:

The story of Betsy Ross as America's matriarch and most famous seamstress is actually — a fabrication. In all likelihood she didn't sew the first flag. The house designated as her residence was actually a bar. And the bones buried in the back yard are probably someone else's. Even the head of Philadelphia's own historical commission dismisses the Betsy Ross tale as pure fiction. But that doesn't stop the city from honoring her this Monday, in a Flag Day celebration, with a fife and drum corps, a mayoral speech and a paid city holiday.

The article then recites many of the details and particulars of the legend, but in a demeaning fashion and with a quote from an expert, Morris Vogel, a history professor at Temple University who, it says, *"thinks the Ross story is preposterous."*

The article further says that the appeal of the Betsy Ross story has made the house itself a strong tourist attraction, second only to the Liberty Bell, but not everybody is enthralled. Quoting further: *"I'd prefer the truth rather than some made-up story,"* says Mollye Upchurch of Oak Ridge, Tennessee, a history major at Ohio Wesleyan University. *"It makes me think how we cover up a lot of American history to evoke that traditional American feeling."* The article concludes:

> *So who did fashion the first flag? The best evidence points to Francis Hopkinson, a lawyer and signer of the Declaration of Independence who also designed seals for several government agencies. That figures, says tourist Terry McGarry, a Philadelphian who considers the Hopkinson theory anti-female; "It knocks another woman out of history." But Barbara Bates, who portrays Betsy Ross on various occasions, insists that the seamstress could have sewn the flag, even if Mr. Hopkinson designed it. "She was a known flag maker who lived right near the Statehouse," she says. "Her husband was the nephew of George Washington's friend, George Ross. She was a businesswoman, she networked."*

From my perspective as a fifth-generation descendant of Betsy, I was appalled when I first read what I felt was an outrageous attack on the family story that I had always accepted as fact. I had to study the issue and determine the facts for myself. This led me to an objective and comprehensive review of published information and opinions regarding the development of our nation's first flag. Keeping an open mind was the first challenge.

The family story was first publicly reported, to the Historical Society of Pennsylvania by her grandson William Canby in 1870. The story was simply this: three men, George Washington, Robert Morris, and her uncle-in-law George Ross had called on Betsy Ross, whose husband John Ross had died only five months earlier, to ask if she would make them a flag. She believed them to be a committee of Congress, but that is not certain. She was not known as a flag maker, but agreed to try. She made some suggestions regarding a design they showed her, including the use of five-pointed instead of six-pointed stars. The flag she made was approved, (she believed by Congress), and she was subsequently paid for making flags for the Pennsylvania Navy.

William Canby, and then his brother George Canby, made a serious attempt to confirm the specifics of the story. The official records of the government from the period were studied, as were other sources of information, and the findings were compiled by George Canby, and published after his death by Dr. Lloyd Balderston in 1909 as "The Evolution of the American Flag."

As I got into this work, it became evident that otherwise competent people had chosen to deny or dismiss the family legend, pointing out the lack of confirmation, such as in the letters of George Washington. I also discovered that these people were unaware of the art of Samuel Waldo and Ellie Wheeler which only came to light in the last 25 years. Further, they did not assign any significance to the art of Charles Willson Peale and Emanuel Leutze. Finally, I have uncovered previously unreported folklore that supplements and corroborates the family story.

In this book, I have taken a fresh look at the sparse factual evidence from the early days, speculated on the artistic record, and introduced the new folklore from outside the family. This should create a useful dialogue on the subject. We can have a more honest and realistic view of Betsy Ross going forward into this new century than was true a hundred years ago. And finally, I seriously question giving Francis Hopkinson any credit for the flag which was adopted June 14, 1777 since his design contribution, while acknowledged at that time by those who would have known of it, is never cited as having been utilized.

Contents

List of Illustrations & Exhibits

Preface

In 1909 Dr. Lloyd Balderston published *"The Evolution of the American Flag"* from materials collected by his uncle the late George Canby. The book had very limited circulation and today is difficult to locate. The book was a follow-up to the talk given by William J. Canby to the Historical Society of Pennsylvania in 1870 in which he related in detail the story of how his grandmother, Elizabeth Claypoole, then known as Betsy Ross, had been called upon by George Washington, Robert Morris, and George Ross who, in her recall, were a committee of the Continental Congress. They were seeking to have a flag made in advance of the time when independence would be declared. All of the documentation then available to support the family story was provided along with the testimonials obtained by William Canby from three women who had heard the story directly from Elizabeth. No claim was made that Betsy designed the first flag, rather that she proposed modifications to the design brought to her, including the use of the five-pointed star.

It should be noted that Elizabeth Griscom Ross was known as "Betsy Ross" only during her years of marriage to John Ross and widowhood prior to her later marriage(s). She became Elizabeth Claypoole with her third marriage in 1783 and was known by that name for the rest of her life; however, for simplicity she is referred to throughout this book as Betsy.

William Canby had researched all available public records looking for evidence that the flag he believed Betsy made came into common use after the Declaration of Independence and before the passage of the Flag Resolution on June 14, 1777.

The basic assumption was that the flag which she produced for the 'committee' was the one which, a year later, was adopted by the Continental Congress. However, the only evidence Canby could find of Betsy's involvement in support of her story was that of her being paid in May 1777 for making "colours" delivered to Captain William Richards, storekeeper for the Pennsylvania Navy. Subsequently, the "new constellation" specified in the Flag Resolution has come to be known as the circle-of-stars flag, and it is the flag associated with Betsy.

After the death of William J. Canby in 1890, the effort to validate the family story fell to his younger brother George. Lloyd Balderston says of his uncle George

Canby that "he read all that had been printed about the history of the flag, examined many old manuscripts, searched through all the periodical literature of the Revolutionary period, examined all the facsimiles and printed copies of Revolutionary documents accessible in the libraries of his native city, and personally scrutinized all the papers in the government archives in Washington which could have any bearing on the early history of the Stars and Stripes. He also engaged the services of a reliable firm in London who make a specialty of library research, to conduct an extensive search among the manuscripts preserved in London, and to examine the captured battle-flags in the museums there."

George Canby is given the credit by Lloyd Balderston for having the material for the book almost completely organized before his untimely death in 1907. It is of interest to note that George Canby was apparently familiar with the writings of Schuyler Hamilton who, in 1887 (his second publication on the flag), leaves us with the impression that two flags evolved in the early days of the Revolution.

Today I am attempting to update the work done by my forebears and take a new look at an old story. The facts remain the same except for the introduction of Francis Hopkinson in the last century into the history of our first flag. Historians who have rejected the Betsy Ross story have identified with Francis Hopkinson, and I will examine his role while presenting new evidence and some interesting speculations regarding the family story, a cherished legend, now confirmed as valid history not to be dismissed as myth, as some have proposed.

— John Balderston Harker

Chapter 1

How Did It All Start?

*H*ow did it all start, the story of Betsy Ross and our nation's first flag? Most people today have no idea of the history of the making of the first flag, c. 1776, and the legend that developed to give the honor to Betsy Ross of Philadelphia, who was trained as an upholsterer and also well known in her time as a flag-maker. However, legends being what they are — most commonly plentiful grains of truth with fanciful trappings — legends merit being looked into!

In 1870, ninety-four years after Betsy is said to have sewn the first flag, William J. Canby brought the story to the attention of the general public. In a speech before the Historical Society of Pennsylvania he told the story of how his grandmother, Elizabeth Claypoole, then known as Betsy Ross, had made the first American flag in 1776. Canby had heard the story from Betsy, herself, when he was a child of eleven, and other family members had confirmed her story. When William Canby chose to make the story public, the basic assumption was that the flag that she made was the one that a year later the Continental Congress adopted in the Flag Resolution of June 14, 1777. It had become common to believe that the resolution had to do with a flag for the new nation even though *the new nation was yet to be established*. Furthermore, it was assumed the design of the flag was clear enough to the men who adopted it, even though no record has been found describing the details of their vision for stars arranged in a *"new constellation."*

The term "new constellation" came to be understood as the stars arranged in a circle, although many variations for star placement developed. The circle arrangement became the standard in paintings by well-known artists of the period, the first being one done by Charles Willson Peale in 1779 titled *George Washington at Princeton* (Exhibit 8). There is a flag behind Washington, who is standing, with six-pointed white stars in a circle. This is likely his *headquarters banner* of that date, there being no stripes on the flag in the picture.

Before he made his speech, William J. Canby researched the available government records, receiving special permission to do so through his connection with the Historical Society of Pennsylvania. He was particularly interested in evidence that the flag that he believed to have been made by his grandmother was in use during the time *between* the Declaration of Independence in July 1776 and the adoption of the flag resolution in June 1777. However, William J. Canby found no mention of flags within those archived records.

As to the flag's design(s), legend is that the 'committee' of three men: George Washington, Robert Morris, and William Ross, uncle-in-law to the young widow Betsy and at that time an aide to George Washington, came to Betsy's upholstery shop and presented her a drawing of a flag. Family legend continues that Betsy suggested it would look better if it were rectangular rather than square, and she suggested that the stars should be five-pointed, not the six-pointed as was common in European designs. Furthermore, she said, the five-pointed stars should be in some symmetrical fashion and not randomly scattered on the field of blue in the canton. Family lore continues that Betsy reported that the men protested that five-pointed stars were far too difficult to easily create, whereby Betsy carefully folded a square of paper, deftly took one snip with her upholster shears, and on the spot created a perfect five-pointed star.

Betsy also reported that Washington took the lead role in their meeting, which would be consistent with his leadership position in the Continental Army, which the other two men respected. The flag design to be produced most likely would have been shown to members of the Continental Congress, but it was Colonel Ross as Representative of the Pennsylvania Committee of Safety who brought her the news that her flag had been accepted. (Later he would become a delegate to the Continental Congress and a signer of the Declaration of Independence.)

Just what the flag Betsy agreed to make looked like is not known. She is reported to have said that after she made her suggestions, Washington drew up a revised flag design for her, quite possibly a flag for the new nation. Not a flag for the army or navy, but for the unified states symbolized by thirteen stars in a circle.

Some seventy-five years later, in 1852, Captain Schuyler Hamilton, an 1839 West Point graduate at age nineteen and descendant of General Philip Schuyler of the Revolutionary War, wrote a lengthy treatise on flags throughout history, and concluded with the observation that our first flag had the thirteen states represented by stars in a circle. He illustrated such a flag but with thirty-one five-pointed stars which would have been the number of states at the time of his writing. His treatise does not attribute the flag design to any particular person or persons.

William Canby, the lecturer, died in 1890. His brother, George Canby, continued his brother's effort to document the family story and prepared the text of a book, *The Evolution of the American Flag*. George Canby died in 1907, and the book was published in 1909 by George's nephew Lloyd Balderston. A page in the Canby/Balderston book that is important to our review of early flag designs (Exhibit 14b) is based on Schuyler Hamilton's publication of 1887, which George Canby would certainly have read. In this (his second publication on the subject of our first flag), Schuyler Hamilton references a flag with thirteen stars arranged in a circle hanging in the State Department, and then goes on to describe how a different, but common form of the arrangement of stars came into being.

> *The drawing of this flag in the State Department shows the thirteen stars arranged in a circle, the emblem of perpetuity; but the soldiers, who like sailors, adhere to their traditions with extreme tenacity, could not forget the old crosses, and arranged the stars so as to preserve the design of the crosses — three stars at the top, three in the middle, three at the bottom, two stars midway between the top and middle row, and two stars between the middle and bottom row. The stars in the rows of two stars rested upon what had been the saltier of St. Andrew, and thus the union of the crosses of St. George and St. Andrew, were indicated on the flag. This was the stars and stripes, or the star-spangled banner of our Revolutionary War (Exhibit 15a).*

Hamilton says this arrangement is an alternate to the circle of stars design he presented in 1852 as our nation's first flag, and it became more widely used.

In *The Evolution of the American Flag*, George Canby is at a loss to explain continuing correspondence between General Washington and the War Board about a flag for the army, and in particular the letter to General Washington from the War Office signed by Richard Peterson and dated May 10, 1779: *"As to colors, we refused them for another reason. The Baron Van Steuben mentioned when he was here that he would settle with your excellency some plan as to the colors — one the Standard of the United States which would be the same throughout the army..."* Canby felt that at the time somebody had forgotten the Flag Resolution and its significance. George Canby apparently did not recognize that the army flag would differ from our national flag, because in *his* lifetime they were one and the same.

Historians make the point that a major difficulty with the family story is that Washington never mentions the meeting with Betsy in his correspondence with respect to a flag for the army. In one of his letters he suggests that the army flag could be a variation on the marine flag that was in common use. The flag the Marine Committee described and adopted did not come into common use, so it would have been another design that Washington was thinking of, the more common flag with the stars in lines.

The three men who called on Betsy included Robert Morris who was chairman of the Secret Committee of the Continental Congress. This committee was charged with preparing for the possibility of war with England. The visit with Betsy was about a month before the Declaration of Independence was adopted, so there may have been some secrecy involved. The essence of the family legend is that she made the circle of stars flag, and this would be consistent with actions taken later that year in developing a flag for the Pennsylvania Navy. The Marine Committee's choice of a flag for the Continental Navy differed from the one Pennsylvania adopted, which set the stage for two flags in use in the early years of our nation.

Thus it is worthwhile to revisit the Betsy Ross family tradition, to reconsider how it fits into our current understanding of the events of the period. More importantly, information not available to the Betsy's second-generation descendants, brothers William and George Canby, nor to her third-generation descendant, Dr. Lloyd Balderston, is introduced into the family records. Thus, what began as an attempt to vindicate the family story, evolved into a comprehensive assessment of both pre-existing and more recent information.

Chapter 2

Two Flags Evolve

To understand the development of our national flag, it is well to keep in mind the governmental structure of the United States evolved slowly from the time of the first Continental Congress in 1775 through the adoption of the Constitution in 1788, and beyond. During this time most national governmental activities took place in Philadelphia, which was also the location of the governing body of the State of Pennsylvania. In fact, both activities often took place in the same building, across the hall from each other, in what is now known as Independence Hall.

Several men in Philadelphia were active in both the state government and the Continental Congress. Benjamin Franklin was President of the State Government until he went to France in September 1776. Robert Morris served both bodies in significant capacities. George Ross, Betsy's uncle-in-law, was a member of the Pennsylvania Committee of Safety in 1775 and 1776. He was appointed to the Continental Congress on July 20, 1776 just after he and the other two men had met with Betsy to arrange for the making of a flag. He later became a signer of the Declaration of Independence and was appointed Judge of Admiralty for Pennsylvania in mid-1776.

The colonists were unhappy with their relations with England, and specifically the English Parliament. The Parliament had been trying to find a means to tax the colonies to support the English forces that protected them, and particularly to recover some of the cost of the French and Indian War. For the colonists, finding a way to work together for the common good without giving up the independence and autonomy of the separate states was the challenge. It is of interest to note that nobody knew at the time of the Revolution just what the final form of the new government would be, if the war was won. In the minds of the many well-educated and independent thinkers it would be based on a new set of principles that were still evolving and unlike any government previously known.

The Meeting House of the Society of Free Quakers (Quakers who had separated from their more Orthodox Meeting to support the Continental Congress) has a marble tablet built into the gable end, fronting on Arch Street. The marble tablet reads:

By General Subscription
for the
FREE QUAKERS
Erected in the YEAR
OF OUR LORD 1783,
of the EMPIRE 8.

In his book *Betsy Ross, Last of Philadelphia's Free Quakers,* Ray Thompson states, *"The reference to 'Empire 8' is one of the few public records that supports the early belief, then prevalent among many citizens, that the United States would ultimately become a new empire."*

Thompson further states, *"It was not until the federal Convention met in Philadelphia three years later and framed the constitution of the United States, that the old 'Empire' idea disappeared."*

An interesting note on the construction of the Meeting House, according to a column in the *Philadelphia Inquirer,* December 1, 1926, "Washington and Franklin contributed to the building fund, as did many other public men who believed the Free Quakers had been wronged by the Orthodox because of their loyalty to country."

During this time each state acted independently in making its flags. For example, in Massachusetts the Pine Tree Flag was adopted by the state in April of 1776. Pennsylvania adopted a state flag on September 18, 1779, a blue flag with the arms of the state worked thereon. It is against this background that we consider the development of a national flag. Scot Guenter (1990) says *"Aside from the use of regimental colors, both by local militia and forces sent from Great Britain, flags do not appear to have been a factor in the everyday life of colonists, with the exception of those whose livelihood was connected with maritime pursuits."* So apart from local militia flags, the earliest flags of concern to the colonists were maritime flags to enable ships to identify each other at sea.

As to the flag for the Pennsylvania Navy, apparently this was still an open question in the second half of 1776. On August 19, 1776, shortly after the Declaration of Independence, Captain William Richards, storekeeper for the Pennsylvania Navy, wrote the Pennsylvania Committee of Safety (Richardson, 1982). *"I hope you have agreed what sort of colors I am to have made for the galleys etc., as they are much wanted."* On October 15, 1776, Captain Richards wrote again, *"The Commodore was with me this morning and says the fleet has not any colors to hoist if they should be called on duty. It is not in my power to get them until there is a design fixed on to make the colors by."* A reasonable question is why this issue came up at all unless Betsy's flag was for Washington's personal use.

Francis Hopkinson, the Representative from New Jersey who would later sign the Declaration of Independence, was intimately involved with naval matters for the Continental Congress during this period. He arrived in Philadelphia on June 28, 1776, to serve in the Continental Congress. On July 12th, he was appointed to the eleven-member Marine Committee. On November 6th, he was appointed to the newly created three-member Continental Naval Board with John Nixon and John Wharton. *"He seems to have served not only as chairman of the Board, but also as its secretary, since many letters sent by the Board are in his handwriting."* (Furlong, 1981).

If we assume the flag Betsy made was not intended as a Marine flag, we may speculate that Francis Hopkinson, as a member of the Marine Committee, began to think of a more impressive design as a flag for naval purposes. Several years later, when he first asks for compensation for his *"Labours of Fancy,"* we learn he claims to have designed a flag, calling it (initially) *"The Flag of the United States,"* and then in subsequent invoices, he called it *"The great Naval Flag of the United States,"* and then simply *"The Naval Flag of the United States."*

He doesn't say when the design was submitted so we can only speculate that it was prior to the Flag Resolution. If he made his proposal in the fall of 1776, he might have preferred a flag to be used by both navies. However, it might have been too complex a design for a naval flag. Even so, it would have been out there for discussion. This would have lead to the letters written by Captain Richards, storekeeper. Captain Richards would be aware of the politics of the situation and thus found it necessary to write as he did in order to seek closure on the question of the design for his ships. When a design was settled upon for the Pennsylvania Navy, Betsy was employed to make the flags.

However, while we may speculate on this, there is no clear evidence that Hopkinson submitted a design at this time. His vision of a *"Flag for the United States"* could well come later and was never acted upon. It is more likely that the Marine Committee already had an acceptable design in front of them and acted upon it with the Flag Resolution. Rabbow (1980) suggests that *"everybody concerned with the flag matter at that moment… knew what this flag looked like… likely because the legislators had a design before them on the table which they approved."*

Hastings (1926) has no argument with the question of *"did Hopkinson design a flag,"* but does not address the question of *"was his design accepted."* He does say, *"There is a tradition that on the original design for the national ensign the stars had six points, and that five-pointed stars were later substituted. On the Hopkinson coat-of-arms are three six-pointed stars."* Given that the Marine Committee's design was not adequately communicated, even though they likely had a sample in front of them, flags were made with various star arrangements including stars arranged in lines, and squares of twelve stars with a thirteenth in the middle. Stars were six-pointed or eight-pointed, while ultimately five-pointed stars became the norm.

As to Hopkinson, while it is clear he provided a design at some point in time, there is no evidence that his design was adopted, **even in his own writings**, or in the arguments about paying him for his artistic endeavors, or in the folklore about him. We believe we know what the Marine Committee had in mind when it acted, based on artistic renditions, but to whom the design can be attributed is not recorded. The Pennsylvania Navy had its flag, and the Continental Congress had its naval flag.

All in all, the artistic evidence which predates the speech by William Canby supports the assertion that Betsy was involved in the design/production of our earliest stars and stripes flag(s). Coupled with the artistic evidence, we have the documentation that she made "colours" for the Pennsylvania Navy. It is clear that she was in the right place at the right time and was known to the right people. Quite possibly, she made the circle-of-stars flag for Washington, and then, because of her connections, was selected to make flags for the Pennsylvania Navy. There could have been discussions about one flag for both fleets, the Continental Navy and the Pennsylvania Navy, which would account for the two letters written by Captain Richards asking, *"has a design been settled on?"* Francis Hopkinson would have been involved in these discussions in committee meetings and in the informality of the coffee houses. However, in the end, we have one flag maker and two designs (with stars in straight lines or circular arrangements with variations on each) being utilized over time. Because the flags were mostly for marine purposes, there is no evidence that a national flag was being considered at the time. Hopkinson may have been thinking in that direction with his design for a *"Flag of the United States"* that he later called a *"Naval Flag,"* but he never asserted that his design was accepted, nor has any supportive folklore evolved.

George Canby may have been correct in believing that the Flag Resolution adopted the flag Betsy made. Robert Morris would be the link as he was part of the "committee" and later was Chairman of the Marine Committee. In time, a national flag appeared but two different flags were beginning to evolve in the minds and eyes of the citizens. Captain Richards had his naval flag. George Washington was still waiting for his Army flag.

The Flag Resolution of June 14, 1777

We celebrate National Flag Day on June 14th, established by an act of Congress in 1949. Before that date, beginning about 1890, there were local and state observances of Flag Day organized to instill in people pride in their heritage. What is generally overlooked is the fact that the flag adopted by the 1777 resolution was primarily for naval purposes, and the "United States" did not yet exist. The truth is, the flag was not being authorized by the Continental Congress as a new flag to symbolize the new Nation, the United States of America, as the Flag Resolution is typically interpreted today.

The Resolution adopted by the eleven-man Marine Committee of the Continental Congress reads as follows: *"Resolved that the Flag of the united states be 13 stripes alternate red and white, that the Union be 13 stars white in a blue field representing a new constellation."* The words "United States" were not capitalized but were written in lower case as "united states." The word "flag" was capitalized as might be appropriate for a proper noun, as was the word "union" referring to the canton (Exhibit 12). While this Resolution was adopted about a year after the Declaration of Independence, the thirteen states were unified only in so far as they were concerned with freeing themselves from English domination. The idea of a national flag was not relevant when the goal of the Continental Congress was a *"union of limited powers between equal sovereign states"* (Crane, 1954).

First Anniversary Celebration

The *Pennsylvania Packet* (a Philadelphia newspaper) printed a full report of the first anniversary celebration of the Declaration of Independence. This report speaks of "colours of the United States." This is only a few weeks after the Flag Resolution is passed on June 14th, 1777. The *Packet* report on July 8th is as follows:

> *Last Friday the 4th of July, being the Anniversary of the Independence of the United States of America, was celebrated in this city with demonstrations of joy and festivity. About noon all the armed ships and gallies in the river were drawn up before the city, dressed in the gayest manner, with "the colours of the United States and streamers displayed". At one o'clock, the yards being properly manned, they began the celebration of the day by a discharge of thirteen cannon from each of the ships, and one from each of the thirteen gallies, in honor of the Thirteen United States. In the afternoon, an elegant dinner was prepared for Congress, to which were invited the President and Supreme Executive Council, and Speakers of the Assembly of this State, the General Officers and Colonels of the Army, and strangers of eminence, and the members of the several Continental Boards in town. The Hessian band of music, taken in Trenton the 20th of December last, [NB date is in error] attended and heightened the festivity with some fine performances suited to the joyous occasion, while a corps of British deserters, taken into the service of the continent by the State of Georgia, being drawn up before the door, filled up the intervals with feux de joie.*

The newspaper account continues:

> *After dinner a number of toasts were drank [sic], all breathing independence, and a generous love of liberty, and commemorating the memories of those brave and worthy patriots who gallantly exposed their lives, and fell gloriously in defense of*

freedom and the righteous cause of their country. Each toast was followed by a discharge of artillery and small arms, and a suitable piece of music by the Hessian band. The Glorious fourth of July was reiterated three times, accompanied with triple discharges of cannon and small arms, and loud huzzas that resounded from street to street through the city. Towards evening several troops of North Carolina forces, which was in town on its way to join the grand army, were drawn up in Second Street, and reviewed by Congress and the General Officers. The evening was closed with the ringing of bells, and at night there was a grand exhibition of fire works, (which began and continued with thirteen rockets) on the Commons, and the city was beautifully illuminated. Everything was conducted with the greatest order and decorum, and the face of joy and gladness was universal. Thus may the fourth of July, that glorious and ever memorable day, be celebrated through America, by sons of freedom, from age to age till time shall be no more. Amen, and Amen.

John Adams to Daughter Abigail

John Adams, the delegate from Massachusetts and Chairman of the War Board wrote a letter to his daughter Abigail on July 5, 1777 describing the event as follows (Adams Family Correspondence, 1963):

In the morning the Delaware frigate, several large gallies, and other continental armed vessels, the Pennsylvania [navy] ships and row gallies and guard boats, were all hawled off in the river, and several of them beautifully dressed in the colours of all nations, displayed about upon the masts, yards and rigging. At one o'clock the ships were all manned, that is, the men were ordered aloft, and arranged upon the tops, yards and shrouds, making a striking appearance of companies of men drawn up in order, in the air.

Adams made no mention of the "colours of the United States" from which we might conclude that his vision of what those colours might be was different from that of the reporter for the *Pennsylvania Packet*. In his letter, Adams further relates how *"the wharves and shores were lined with a great concourse of people, all shouting and huzzing, in a manner which gave great joy to every friend of this country"*, but made no mention of a United States flag.

We can well imagine that the average soldier and sailor on the waterfront saw a marine flag they could identify with, although the reporter for the *Pennsylvania Packet* may have been premature in calling it the flag of the United States. It was not the flag that John Adams and the other members of the War Board had approved only a few weeks earlier. John Adams would have had a different naval flag in his mind's eye, one that represented the Continental Navy and at some future time the still developing United States, not just the Pennsylvania Navy. Two flags came into existence in 1776-1777.

Chapter 3

The Symbolic Flag

The earliest flag said to represent the united colonies was hoisted by John Paul Jones aboard the *Alfred,* a naval vessel, in the harbor of Philadelphia. Jones wrote to Robert Morris with pride that *"it is my good fortune, as the senior of the first Lieutenants, to hoist myself the Flag of America the first time it was displayed."* This was about a month before the Grand Union flag was flown on Prospect Hill, Somerville, (then part of Charlestown) on January 1, 1776. The flag Jones flew was likely the Grand Union flag, suggesting that it was a design adopted about this time by unknown, but important people and carried by Washington to his headquarters in Cambridge.

The Grand Union flag was an easy modification of the British Red Ensign under which colonial soldiers had marched shoulder to shoulder with British troops in a century of frontier wars. Red and white stripes in flags were not new, and in this instance to make the British Red Ensign into an American flag simply involved sewing six white stripes over the red field. This produced the thirteen red and white stripes that symbolized the number and union of the colonies. It was called the "Grand Union" flag because the British crosses remained in the upper left quarter, which symbolized a continuing allegiance to the crown while the stripes expressed American determination to achieve full rights and status within the Empire.

This flag was in use until the signing of the Declaration of Independence, and according to Scot Guenter (1990), John Jay wrote a letter on July 1776 noting that as Congress had not as yet made any order concerning continental colors, captains of armed vessels followed their own fancies. This condition continued for some time, with the only constant element being thirteen stripes.

Although the Flag Resolution implies a specific arrangement of the stars, the specifications were not given and so any arrangement could be called a "new constellation." As a result a number of different designs developed. Among the alternatives, the circle of stars was an infrequent choice in the period immediately after the Declaration of Independence. The variations that appeared involved the arrangement of the stars in the canton, the number of points on the stars, and the inclusion of blue stripes along with the red and white stripes.

It was three years later when Hopkinson first presented a bill for services rendered, including, as first on the list of artistic (Fancy) work, his claim relative to doing a design for "The Flag of the United States". In two subsequent iterations of his bill, his design was described as a naval flag. Hopkinson's claim to having designed a flag is not in dispute, but the question is, *"what became of his design?"* At about the time he submitted his bill for services, the flag with an eagle in the canton and a crest of stars comes into use.

In submitting his bill for services, Hopkinson does not claim any credit for his design being adopted in June 1777. The most obvious answer to the question "what became of his design" is that it was not adopted by the Marine Committee. Instead, some other flag design was adopted which, as later evidence reveals, had a circle of thirteen stars. The symbolism of the design was not lost on the artists of the period, even though it was not utilized as a practical flag.

To whom goes the credit for the "Circle of Stars" flag design? To the Marine Committee (of which Robert Morris was Chairman), to George Washington, to Betsy Ross or to Francis Hopkinson? It is impossible to assign credit with any certainty. The earliest artistic representation of the circle of stars is a picture done by Charles Willson Peale in 1779 entitled *George Washington at Princeton* showing Washington's Headquarters banner with thirteen six-pointed stars in a circle, white on the blue field (Exhibit 8). These stars are consistent with Washington's personal Coat of Arms. According to Richardson, Washington's Headquarters banner of 1781 has six-pointed stars arranged 3-2-3-2-3 .

A recent government publication, *Our Flag*, September 21, 2001, states *"The flag popularly known as the 'Betsy Ross flag' which arranged the stars in a circle, did not appear* (in use) *until the early 1790s."* The publication does not state where or how it came into use, but a variation of it may have flown in Philadelphia as part of the Grand Federal Procession in 1788 celebrating the adoption of the Constitution.

Hopkinson wrote a very detailed account of the celebration, which he helped organize and participated in as judge of the Admiralty. In his account of the order of the procession he reports that among the early elements in the parade were:

The consuls and representatives of foreign states in alliance with America, in an ornamented car drawn by four horses.

This is followed by a single line regarding the next in the line of march:

Capt. Thomas Bell with the flag of the United States of America.

Since the flag was not described further, we do not know if it was the circle of stars flag or a variation on it. A common design had twelve stars arranged in a circle and the thirteenth in the center and it could have been this. Such an image, but with six-pointed stars, was part of the flag carried by the Society of Pewterers in the Constitution Parade in New York on July 23, 1788 (Richardson 1982). Whatever design the flag makers chose to represent the stars and stripes, we do know the circle of stars design had taken hold as a symbol of the unity and perpetuity of the thirteen states drawn together under the new constitution.

The European View

We have noted that some designs included blue stripes although these are not mentioned in the Flag Resolution. They were favored by John Paul Jones. In Europe, Benjamin Franklin wrote to the King of the Two Sicilies that our nation's flag had red, white and blue stripes. When Franklin left Philadelphia in September of 1776 to go to France, there was no agreed-upon national naval flag. Dispatches from Philadelphia to Paris may not have mentioned the Flag Resolution in June of 1777.

Franklin could have been influenced by John Paul Jones, who spent considerable time with him in Paris while waiting for command of a ship. Jones favored a flag with stripes in three colors; when Jones was given command of the *Bonhomme Richard* he flew a flag with red, white, and blue stripes. Its canton had eight-pointed stars arranged 4-5-4. The thirteen stripes begin with a blue stripe at the top followed by one of red and one of white. The red and white repeat again before another blue stripe comes in adjacent to the bottom of the blue canton. Next came a red and white stripe followed by a red, a blue, and a white. This flag was transferred to the *Serapis* after the famous sea battle off Flamborough Head, England, in which the *Bonhomme Richard* was lost. In the early years, European representations of the flag (as on naval recognition flag sheets) were influenced by the John Paul Jones' flag and showed blue stripes.

The *Alliance*, which accompanied him in the battle with the *Serapis*, had brought Lafayette home in 1779. It flew a flag with red and white stripes with a white stripe at the top and bottom, and eight-pointed stars arranged 3-2-3-2-3. Both flags were painted at the time by a Dutch artist while the ships were in the Dutch harbor of Texel. Clearly, there was no single naval flag at this time. Since many of the flags in use were made by the sailmaker on a ship, variations such as a white stripe on the top and bottom occurred, and six- or eight-pointed stars were regularly used since the trick or technique of making five-pointed stars wasn't widely known.

Regardless of the variations that appeared in practical use, a *symbolic* flag gradually impressed itself on the consciousness of the people in the colonies.

Chapter 4

Regimental Colors

Having established that a variety of naval flags were in existence early in the nation's development, we can turn to army regimental flags. Washington wanted each regiment to be readily identified by its own flag. A few of these survive. In 1907, Gherardi Davis published a limited-edition book of color plates and descriptive information on state regimental flags. He found that only a few flags existed from New Hampshire, Rhode Island, Connecticut, New York, and Pennsylvania. He also mentions a painting of Washington by Peale (Exhibit 8), that has a flag in the background, and he says, *"The stars are, strange to say, six-pointed."* In 1907 the five-pointed star had long been the norm. Davis does not recognize that the image in the background is Washington's Headquarters banner.

Most all of the regimental flags had cantons with a relevant image in it. Talmadges's Dragoons of Connecticut is represented by two different standards, one pink and one blue, both with a canton having 13 stripes. The Westmoreland County Battalion has a flag with the English Jack on the upper right corner. The canton on the Philadelphia Light Horse flag (which existed before the war) originally had the British Union in the canton, according to Furlong (1981), but this was painted over with silver stripes to represent the thirteen colonies.

In his 1907 publication, Davis records that the colors of the 2nd New Hampshire regiment were captured and are in the possession of Colonel George W. Rogers, Wykeham, Burgess Hill, Sussex, England. They are described as being silk, about five feet by five feet six inches, in size; one blue and one buff. The blue flag has the British crosses in the canton, the buff flag has eight triangles of red and blue arranged to form two crosses.

At the close of the war, a regiment of Black soldiers known then as "Bucks of America" was given a flag, the canton of which had thirteen five-pointed stars (Exhibit 13a).

Of special interest are the Rhode Island 1st Regiment and 2nd Regiment flags. The remnants of these flags are in the State House in Providence, having been presented to the state at the close of the war in 1784. This likely accounts for their existence today. They are described by Howard M. Chapin (1925), both flags having blue cantons with white (in one case) and gold (in the other) five-pointed stars arranged 3-2-3-2-3. The cantons are painted on the silk flag.

The 1st and 2nd Rhode Island regiments were recruited in the spring of 1777, although Rhode Islanders had been part of the action since 1775. As regiments, they had silk flags with emblems on them specific to their Rhode Island origins. One of these flags is specifically mentioned in the *National Geographic* (Exhibit 13b). The flag has a canton painted on it with five-pointed stars arranged 3-2-3-2-3, the canton being set in from the edge of the flag. Chapin writes, *"The reason for this peculiarity in regard to the field and the canton is that in the early flags the canton was painted and so comparatively stiff and quite different from the dyed silk of the rest of the field, the flexible quality of which was needed where the flag was attached to the staff, usually being wound once around it."*

The pictured regimental flag has a fouled blue anchor on a white field, with "Hope" in blue above it. There are no stripes. Richardson (1982) acknowledges *"the above standard could have originally been that of the Rhode Island 1st Regiment of 1777 and carried by the combined Regiment of 1781 as one of its two colors."* [The 1st and 2nd Regiments had been combined into one under Lt. Colonel Olney from May 1781 to November 1783, due to the reduction in their numbers.]

Some historians believe that this design originated with the Rhode Islanders, but they could have known of it from serving with Washington through the fall and early winter of 1776, before their enlistments were up and they went home. If Betsy produced flags with this canton-design for the Pennsylvania Navy, the design would have been noted by many people and talked about by the men in the ranks. The Rhode Islanders who served with Washington in 1776 comprised the core of the regiments organized in the spring of 1777. Thus it is an open question as to whether or not Rhode Islanders can lay claim to having originated it.

Chapter 5

Charles H. Weisgerber, the Artist
A True Believer

The legend surrounding Betsy Ross, while based on the story told by William J. Canby in his speech in 1870, was greatly enhanced by the painting by Charles H. Weisgerber in 1893 titled *Birth of Our Nation's Flag*, which was exhibited at the Columbian Exposition of 1893 in Chicago. Weisgerber won the $1,000 prize offered by the City of Philadelphia in 1890 for a painting that would depict a historical event associated with the city.

How the painting came into being is told in the website of the State Museum of Pennsylvania.

In 1891, as a young artist just returning to Philadelphia from studies in Paris, Weisgerber heard [the Betsy Ross story] from the owner of the former site of Betsy Ross's Arch Street upholstery shop. From his grandson, Charles H. Weisgerber II, we have the statement that "in the store front window a sign stated that in this building the first American Flag was made by Betsy Ross. That day Weisgerber was inspired to do the research with William Canby for the ideas that created in his mind the vision of Betsy Ross presenting the flag to George Washington."

His painting (Exhibit 5) reflects the story told by William Canby of a "committee" of George Washington, William Ross, and Robert Morris calling on Betsy regarding the making of a flag, and it shows her with the finished product on her lap, with thirteen five-pointed stars in a circle. In 1952, the United States Postal Service issued a stamp commemorating the 200th birthday of Betsy Ross, using a greatly reduced image of the painting (Exhibit 25 & 26a).

To understand how Betsy Ross became our national heroine, it is important to understand the mood of the country in the late 1800s and the beginning of the decade of the 1890s (Scot Guenter, 1990). Numerous patriotic organizations were established from 1875 on, which were all hereditary (opposite page).

There was a pride in the nation we had become, and established citizens differentiated themselves from the large immigrant population that was being absorbed. Focusing on the flag served to cement diverse people into one nation. The Pledge of Allegiance to the Flag was introduced into the schools in 1892 and became a part of the daily curriculum. In 1896 John Philip Sousa composed his most popular and enduring work, "The Stars and Stripes Forever."

During the two years prior to the Spanish-American War, a custom had spread of seated audiences rising in the presence of the national flag when it passed on review (Guenter, 1990). *The patriotic fervor of the 1890s resulted in America entering the twentieth century with an assortment of flag rituals and uses far more complex than that of the society only fifty years earlier.* Poems, songs, stories and legends were created; *"The cult of the flag had secured the national banner the highest honor in the constellation of patriotic symbols employed in the culture."* In Minnesota, the Daughters of the American Revolution promoted proper flag etiquette and the raising of flags on schoolhouses and public buildings. The chapter in Fergus Falls in central Minnesota, an area with a large population of Scandinavians, devoted themselves to this task, concerned that not much attention was being paid to these observances.

Thus, whatever our country of origin, we were all "Americans" although descendants of the earliest of the immigrants regarded themselves as more "American" than some others. For example, in Boston, "Irish Need Not Apply" often accompanied signs inviting job applicants.

The patriotic trend in the period leading up to the Spanish-American War proved especially timely for the story of Betsy Ross and the flag. The 'circle of stars' flag was already our symbolic flag because of its use in artistic scenes of the Revolution, so when she is shown with that flag, whether or not she produced the flag for George Washington, she became identified with it.

The Weisgerber painting had been in storage for a number of years when JoAnn Menezes, an art historian (1997) contacted the descendants and encouraged them

Colonial and National Original and Hereditary Patriotic Organizations
Source: A. G. Weaver, *The Story of the Our Flag 1898*

COLONIAL AND NATIONAL. 91

ORIGINAL AND HEREDITARY PATRIOTIC

ORGANIZATIONS.

Instituted.	Title of Organization.	Classification.
1783.	Society of the Cincinnati.	Hereditary.
1805.	New England Society.	Original and Hereditary.
1847.	St. Nicholas Society of N. Y.	Hereditary.
1847.	Aztec Club of 1847.	Original and Hereditary.
1875.	Sons of the American Revolution.	Hereditary.
1875.	Sons of the Revolution.	Hereditary.
1875.	St. Nicholas Club of New York City.	Hereditary.
1883.	Huguenot Society of America.	Hereditary.
1885.	Holland Society of New York.	Hereditary.
1890.	Daughters of the American Revolution.	Hereditary.
1890.	Colonial Dames of America (a).	Hereditary.
1890.	Naval Order of the U. S.	Original and Hereditary.
1891.	Daughters of the Revolution.	Hereditary.
1892.	Society of the War of 1812.	Hereditary.
1892.	United States Daughters.	Hereditary.
1892.	Society of Colonial Wars.	Hereditary.
1893.	Colonial Dames of America (b).	Hereditary.
1894.	Mil. Order of Foreign Wars.	Original and Hereditary.
1894.	Colonial Order.	Hereditary.
1894.	Daughters of the Cincinnati.	Hereditary.
1894.	Society of the Mayflower Descendants.	Hereditary.
1895.	Order of Washington.	Hereditary.
1895.	Daughters of Holland Dames.	Hereditary.
1895.	Society of New England Women.	
		Hereditary and non-Hereditary.
1895.	Colonial Society	Hereditary.
1895.	Children of the American Revolution.	Hereditary.
1896.	Order of the Founders and Patriots of America.	Hereditary.
1896.	Order of the Old Guard (uniformed).	Hereditary.
1896.	Dames of the Revolution.	Hereditary.
1896.	Colonial Daughters of the 17th Century.	Hereditary.
1896.	Order of the Descendants of Colonial Governors.	Hereditary.
1896.	Holland Dames of New Netherlands.	Hereditary.
1896.	League of the Red, White and Blue (children).	Non-Hereditary.
1897.	America's Founders and Defenders.	Hereditary.
1897.	Society of American Wars.	Original and Hereditary.
1896.	American Flag Association.	Mixed.
	Daughters of Liberty.	
	Patriotic League of the Revolution.	
	George Washington Memorial Association.	
	St. Nicholas Society of Nassau Island.	Hereditary.

to have it restored. While in her view it is not great art, it is historically important. The scene, as staged by the artist, is not the one described by the Canbys. According to Menezes, *"It is a representation of a carefully constructed, larger than life image of the entirety of that story."* Weisgerber copied portraits of the three men to lend his painting authenticity. He painted Betsy based on a composite of her daughters and granddaughters to approximate her actual appearance. Menezes writes:

> *In Weisgerber's construction, all of (Canby's) story elements are compressed into a single miraculous moment. The committee is present as the flag is born. Betsy has made the prototype flag and it is being delivered. Washington extends his hand toward Ross's wondrous gift. Although the Honorable George Ross and Robert Morris are also present on this occasion, and while they too looked pleased, they do not share the intimate moment with Betsy and George.*

> *The "Birth of our Nation's Flag" not only told the story of the origin of the national colors, it also introduced Betsy Ross to the American public. It was this image that propagated the story of the Philadelphia needlewoman and constructed the Betsy Ross myth in its own terms. In this image Betsy Ross is elevated to her position of national prominence as an historic figure - the mother of the new nation because this picture not only constructs an historic moment, it also creates an icon. Betsy Ross is not just the seamstress who assembled the original flag; in this painting she becomes the mother of the national emblem which is the sacred symbol of the United States.*

Weisgerber's painting was exhibited in the Pennsylvania Pavilion at the Chicago Columbian Exposition in 1893 where it enjoyed considerable public acclaim. This encouraged Charles Weisgerber, who had a vision to acquire and preserve the house. He organized an association of prominent Philadelphians to help him in the solicitation of funds to achieve this goal. He was joined by John Quincy Adams of New York (descendant of two Presidents of the United States), who took over as Secretary of the fund-raising effort, and the two formed the American Flag House and Betsy Ross Memorial Association. Two million chromolithographs of a membership certificate were printed as Certificates of Membership (Exhibit 24) and in 1898 the fund-raising began. This method of obtaining funds from the masses was a new concept in those days.

The Certificates of Membership were sold for ten cents apiece. Early returns from this promotion exceeded $80,000. The house was purchased for $25,000, saving this historic property at a time when many others were being torn down. The Memorial Association took over the house in 1898 whereupon the Weisgerbers moved in. In 1905 the association offered the property to Congress, but because of controversy surrounding the funding mechanism and a lack of real authentication of either the house or the story, the offer was declined.

This was a very passionate time in the coming of age of our nation. We were still only one or two lifetimes away from the Revolutionary War and the events of that period were being recalled. With this, Betsy Ross became something of a Founding Mother symbol. The fund-raising effort, initiated in Philadelphia, was imitated by at least one patriotic group of women. In Minneapolis, a group organized as the Elizabeth Ross Monument Association to build a monument to her. I came into possession of a letter regarding this fund-raising effort. This letter, addressed to the Custer Corp. #15, in Carson City, Nevada, is undated but the envelope is postmarked July 19, 1899. The Hennepin County Historical Society in Minneapolis has no record that anything came of this, but the intent was to erect the first monument to a woman.

The Philadelphia fund-raising was not without controversy, according to newspaper articles of the day. (Files: The American Flag House and Betsy Ross Memorial). Two Philadelphia newspapers, the *North American* and the *Inquirer* were both looking over the shoulders of the men raising the money. After the initial flurry of activity with over $80,000 raised in Pennsylvania, the papers began to ask where the money was going. By June of 1900, the Officers and Directors of the Association decided to ask for an accounting. Dr. Edward Brooks, President of the Association and Superintendent of Public Schools, called on John Quincy Adams, Secretary, to account for every cent which had passed through his hands.

The accounting was made, and it appeared that the cost of the certificates, mailing tubes, and clerical expense was about three cents per subscription, leaving seven cents for the organizers. Just where that money went was not explained. Secretary Adams is quoted by the *North American* as saying, "*I am conducting the affairs of this association as I would conduct a private enterprise. Its details concern no one except the officers of the association.*" This brought the Governor of Pennsylvania into the picture, asking for a probe into the finances in light of the fact that a significant sum of money had poured into the Association from Pennsylvania citizens. No further explanation was given.

While Adams resisted revealing just how much money was raised by the solicitation, the *Inquirer* reported on December 14, 1901 that the Board of Directors refused to reinstate Weisgerber to the Board. He was the manager and custodian of the Betsy Ross House and apparently had taken exception to a number of actions of the Board. The article reports that John Quincy Adams pulled the enraged Weisgerber aside and advised him, *"You have a little business here selling copies of your picture and postal cards, so there may be some dissent about reinstatement at this time. Wait a year."*

John Quincy Adams remained active in the fund-raising until his death in January 1911. The receipts from the continued sale of the membership certificate and other souvenir items sustained the Weisgerber family in the Betsy Ross house. A son was born to the Weisgerbers in 1902, in the Betsy Ross house, and was named "Vexil Domus" which is Latin for flag house.

Weisgerber and his wife lived in the house as curators until his death in 1932. His vision was to develop the house as a central, public place for ceremonies. His son continued as curator but the house was declining until A. Atwater Kent acquired it in 1937 and undertook its restoration. The house was deeded to the City of Philadelphia on June 23, 1941. The famous painting is now on permanent display at the State Museum of Pennsylvania in Harrisburg. The efforts of Charles Weisgerber and John Quincy Adams saved the house, and inspired the image of Betsy Ross.

Yet it was not enough for Charles Weisgerber that he saved the house. He was responsible for acquiring the open space adjoining the house. On Flag Day, June 14, 1929, he announced, *"The four properties west of the Betsy Ross House, covering 7,500 square feet on the side and rear, and 110 feet in depth, have been secured and will be torn down to safeguard the birthplace of 'Old Glory' from fire, and provide space in which to hold patriotic services."* This space has been put to good use, including bringing the remains of Betsy and John Claypoole from almost forgotten graves and re-interring them in the Courtyard.

It was firmly believed, and it was incorporated into grade school text books, that Betsy made our first flag, referred to here as our nation's "symbolic" flag, and that the term "new constellation", a term the Continental Congress applied to an

To Leo J. Fleury
Burlington, Vermont

Vexil Domus Weisgerber, Curator

FIRST DAY OF ISSUE *Betsy Ross House*
Philadelphia.
Pennsylvania

THREE CENT

BETSY ROSS COMMEMORATIVE STAMP

HONORING THE 200TH ANNIVERSARY

OF THE

BIRTH OF THE MAKER OF THE

FIRST AMERICAN FLAG

BETSY ROSS HOUSE
PHILADELPHIA, PA.

JANUARY SECOND, NINETEEN FIFTY-TWO
ELEVEN A.M.

unspecified arrangement of the thirteen stars, is represented by the flag in the Weisgerber picture. This arrangement of stars had been used in pictures by important artists since immediately after the Revolutionary War, and as late as the famous *"Spirit of '76"* painted in 1876 by Archibald M. Willard, the original of which hangs in the Marblehead (Massachusetts) Town Hall, in the Selectmen's Room (Exhibit 27b). A particularly well-known use was by Emanuel Leutze in his 1851 painting, "Washington Crossing the Delaware".

There is folklore evidence recently uncovered (discussed later) to support the view that the flag Betsy made for Washington was the circle of starts flag with five-pointed stars. We know nothing of Betsy's work until 1777 when she is paid for making "co-lours" for the Pennsylvania Navy. These could have had the stars arranged in the 3-2-3-2-3 pattern, a simple transition from the British Crosses in the Grand Union flag.

Francis Hopkinson may have submitted a design at this time, but it is equally possible that his design was submitted several years later, when it was somewhat more clear that there would be a "United States" for which a flag might be important. So while there is no dispute that he presented one, it is not known when this was, or what it was. Most important, there is no claim on his part, and no folklore or hearsay recall to suggest that it was adopted.

On the other hand, the flag adopted by the Marine Committee for the Continental Navy, while attractive symbolically, was impractical as a naval flag and did not serve Washington's objectives of a flag for the Army. It can be argued that the Pennsylvania Navy flag evolved into the Star Spangled Banner, and ultimately into our national flag. The circle of stars flag, as painted by Weisgerber, had become the symbolic flag of the United States.

Chapter 6

Betsy Ross, Quaker Rebel

Betsy Ross, as shown in public records, was well known in Philadelphia, just as would be expected for a Quaker businesswoman. Known for honesty, fair pricing, and careful crafts work, Quaker businesses flourished in the old and new worlds alike. Whereas all women of that era were expected to be able to do needlework or to sew a fine seam, Betsy took this one step further by apprenticing herself to John Webster, an upholsterer. As with any service industry, business owners and workers would become known for their skill in rendering requests. Therefore, it is of no surprise that Betsy would be approached by the 'committee' of three seeking to have a flag design sewn rather quickly. The fact she was the newly widowed niece-in-law of one of the men simply confirms the taking-care-of-one's-own philosophy seen throughout history. Having been raised Quaker, but having been 'read-out-of-meeting' for marrying outside her faith, it is no surprise that Betsy would likely have been willing to support the new Independence movement that split her Quaker community and not be supportive of the British officers who quartered in her house. Furthermore, Betsy is said to have been called the "Little Rebel" by the British — a name which she justified in many ways with her independent nature, her career choice, her religious choices, supporting herself as a widow and in hiring other women to work with her.

Regarding ownership of her shop, there is no doubt Betsy was, as her family claims, fully capable and responsible for her upholstery shop. In *Betsy Ross, the Griscom Legacy*, Timmins and Yarrington (1983) note that the 1791 *Philadelphia Directory* of Clement Biddle lists Betsy's third husband John Claypoole, upholsterer, at 80 South Second Street. At that time, John had a position with the Custom House, so this listing can be construed as representing the family business with the business in the husband's name. But by 1830, Betsy was listed in her own right. Ray Thompson (1972) records that the city directory of the 1830s listed: *"Elizabeth Claypoole, Upholsterer, 74 South Front Street."* However, Thompson adds that Betsy gave up active work on the business in 1827 so the 1830 listing represents her ongoing family business.

As for Betsy's physical appearance, Betsy is described by a great niece, who as a child lived with her mother in Betsy's house, as being a beautiful little old lady with very blue eyes. She recalled her Aunt Elizabeth as having made her living making cushions and flags for the ships on the Delaware. It is said that her daughter and granddaughter resembled her, so that later, when artists sought models, they chose those women to portray a younger Betsy [Exhibits 29 a & b]. In his book, *Betsy Ross, Quaker Rebel (1930)*, Edwin Satterthwaite Parry (a direct descendant) provides an interesting picture of growing up in Philadelphia before and after the Revolutionary War. The illustrations in the book are by J. L. G. Ferris [Exhibit 7]. The following section is abstracted from that book with additions from the records of the Society of Free Quakers.

Abstract from Parry's "Betsy Ross, Quaker Rebel"

Betsy was born on January 1, 1752 (the day the Gregorian calendar was adopted), on the family farm in New Jersey across the river from Philadelphia. She was the sixth of the nine children of Samuel and Rebecca Griscom who survived to adulthood. Before she was five, they had moved to Philadelphia where four generations of the Griscom family had lived and played an important role in building the city. She grew up in a community in which the Quakers were a major, if not majority group. She was educated in Quaker schools, as was the custom of the day for both girls and boys, and we can presume she was a demure young Quaker maiden in the plain dress of the Quakers. Following Quaker school, Betsy was apprenticed to John Webster, a master upholsterer from London who had established himself in Philadelphia (Exhibit 32).

According to Parry, Betsy was attractive and personable, and was courted by three young men: John Ross, an apprentice in the same upholstery shop as Betsy; Joseph Ashburn, a ship's captain; and John Claypoole, a tanner. The first two were not of her faith and the last, John Claypoole, while of an old Quaker family, was no longer a practicing Quaker. His grandfather James Claypoole had come to America from Norborough, England, in 1683. He was a wealthy merchant and a close associate of William Penn's. John Ross's father married an Episcopalian, Elizabeth Hall, and became an Episcopal clergyman. Joseph Ashburn was a ship captain who sailed a small merchant vessel owned by his aunt. Of these three, we can presume that Betsy's family would have favored John Claypoole, but her choice was John Ross, whose uncle, George Ross, would later play a major role in her life.

On November 4, 1773, Betsy and John Ross eloped across the Delaware River to Hugg's Tavern in Gloucester, New Jersey to marry. Young couples were required to post a bond as to their being of age (21) to marry. The wedding certificate held by the Gloucester County (New Jersey) Historical Society, reveals that William Hugg, Jr. a close friend of John Ross, signed the bond along with the justice of the peace, James Bowman, who performed the ceremony. The tavern no longer exists, but its huge fireplace in front of which the wedding may have been performed was saved and reconstructed in the Hunter-Lawrence-Jessup Museum of the Gloucester County Historical Society.

The couple did not announce their marriage until the spring of 1774 when their housekeeping plans were complete. As can be imagined, this created quite a stir among her family and the Quakers of her Meeting when they learned that Betsy was the bride of a man outside of her faith. Edwin Parry writes, *"In the minute book of the Philadelphia Monthly Meeting, Northern District, of the year 1774, under date of Fourth Month [April] 26, we read that a committee of Women Friends has treated with Elizabeth Ross, late Griscom, on account of her marriage with a person of another religious persuasion contrary to the advice of her parents and the good order used among us, and she does not appear inclined to repent or condemn her breach of duty. In this manner the wheels of excommunication were set in motion."*

For Betsy there followed an interval when she was outside the Quaker community. During this period she attended Christ Church (Episcopalian) where a pew still has a plaque on it bearing her name. An adjacent pew was later used by George Washington. Betsy attended Christ Church c. 1774, and George Washington, attended in 1790-1797 when he lived in Philadelphia during his Presidency.

With the news from Lexington Green and Concord in April 1775, the second Continental Congress declared that war was now an actual fact, and Philadelphia became the pivotal point of revolutionary activity. John Ross cast his lot with the patriot cause. As one of a company of citizen guards, John guarded military supplies brought from the West Indies. It was in this activity that he became ill.

The details of John's illness and death are found in Timmins (1983). He reports that William Canby wrote a letter on February 21, 1870 to a gentleman named William Read who was preparing family records and family history and who was interested in John Ross as a relative by marriage.

Canby stated that he had talked with his mother, who *"remembered her mother [Betsy Ross] saying that [the men] were taking exercise in jumping and lifting and throwing weights to keep warm; in consequence of which he had a hemorrhage and afterwards became insane for a time. John was deranged for about 18 months when he died having been married just two years.... He wrote immense quantities of senseless matter thinking he was composing some important work."*

Ross family records show that Sarah Leech, John's mother, lost her mind and presumably died insane. There is a report that John's death was due to an explosion at the docks, but this is likely a later fabrication to conceal the insanity. No documentation of an explosion has ever been found, according to Timmins.

Henry Moeller (2003) offers a possible insight regarding John's illness and death. John Webster, the upholsterer to whom John Ross and Betsy were apprenticed, advertised in the *Pennsylvania Journal*, August 20, 1767. In the quaint manner of the times, he stated that he had had the honor of working with applause for several of the nobility and gentry of England and Scotland and that he hoped that he would meet with a small degree of encouragement among the benevolent in Philadelphia. Then he wrote (after giving his address), *"N.B. At the same place may be had Webster's Liquor, for entirely destroying that offensive and destructive vermin called Buggs, which he has completed with success."*

Moeller speculates that John Ross may have been expected to formulate this early pesticide (i.e., *"Webster's Liquor"*), and his exposure to it might have caused his poor health and eventual death. The ingredients are not known.

At the time, Betsy's faithfulness in caring for John, and his family connections to many prominent people, would have endeared Betsy to them. We can only speculate as to how this might have lead to her becoming involved in making the first flag not too many months later. What we do know is that after her husband died, Betsy, who was just past her 24th birthday, busied herself with their upholstery business, and possibly with the assistance of some of her sisters, was able to manage without the help, it is said, that her father offered.

Soon Betsy was being courted by Captain Ashburn. He was heavily involved in bringing in supplies from the West Indies but found time to marry her on June 15th, 1777. Coincidentally, this was the day after the Flag Resolution was passed.

By September 1777, Cornwallis occupied Philadelphia. In October, John Claypoole, Betsy's third suitor, now a second Lieutenant in Washington's army, was wounded at the battle of Germantown when Washington attempted to drive Cornwallis out of Philadelphia. Later, after participating in several other significant battles, John Claypoole resigned from the army at the end of his enlistment because the wound he had suffered made it difficult for him to stand long marches over rough terrain.

Betsy's second husband, Captain Ashburn and others were keeping their boats out of sight of the British up the Delaware River, but when Cornwallis finally abandoned Philadelphia in May 1778, Washington ordered the small fleet scuttled to keep the boats out of the hands of the British. The Captain returned home to Betsy, and in September 1779 their baby daughter Aucilla (Zilla) was born. Unfortunately she died when young.

When the port opened again, Captain Ashburn took command of a new, larger ship and sailed down the Delaware Bay for the West Indies. It should have been an easy six to eight week voyage. At about the same time, John Claypoole, who had decided to try the sea for a living, shipped out of Philadelphia as a seaman on a large transatlantic merchant vessel bound for France to deliver a cargo and return with supplies for the military.

Both vessels were commissioned as privateers with authorization to take British ships as prizes. As fate would have it, both ships were captured by the British. Betsy was at home expecting another child, her daughter Eliza, who was born in February of 1781 but there was no word of her Captain Ashburn, and none of John Claypoole and his shipmates.

It was common practice for the British to try to enlist captured sailors in the service of the King. Failing this, the men would be kept on ships until they could be put ashore in England, and so it came about that Claypoole found himself confined in Old Mill Prison in Plymouth, England. He arrived there in July 1781, and was astonished to recognize Ashburn in a group brought to the prison some time later. Throughout this period, neither Betsy nor the Claypoole family had any word about their men. In prison the two men were close friends until Joseph Ashburn died of an unnamed malady in March 1782. Betsy was again a widow, but she would not know this until late in August 1782 when John Claypoole was released from prison and returned home with the news of the death of her husband.

John Claypoole went to sea again, making another voyage to France from which he returned safely, and upon his return proposed marriage to Betsy. On May 8, 1783, they were joined in matrimony. She was now thirty years old. During the years that followed, Betsy ran an upholstering and flag making-business and had women working for her. Five daughters were born to the couple, one of whom died in infancy. John Claypoole worked in the Custom House until his wartime disability undermined his health. He died August 3, 1817 at the age of 65.

Philadelphia Inquirer: The "Free Quakers"

A column in the December 1, 1926 edition of the *Philadelphia Inquirer*, on the 150th anniversary of the beginning of the Revolution, reports that, for supporting the cause of liberty, *"Orthodox Friends had early on disowned Timothy Matlack, quickly followed by his brother White Matlack, Samuel Wetherill, Christopher Marshall, Dr. Benjamin Say, Clement and Owen Biddle, William Crispin, Joseph Warren, Moses Bartram, and Isaac Howell."* Early in 1781 eight of these men organized themselves into a Quaker Meeting and invited any others *"who had been disowned for **Matters Religious or Civil** to join them."* They became *"The Monthly Meeting of Friends, called by some **The Free Quakers**."* Membership roles indicate fifty to sixty people joined the group by the end of 1781. John and Elizabeth Claypoole became members in 1785 (Wetherill, 1894).

The "Free Quakers", as some called them, came into being as a result of differences within the Quaker Meeting as to desirability of supporting the Continental Congress in opposition to the King. In Charles Wetherill's 1894 history of the *"Free Quakers"* he explains the attitudes that divided the Quaker community. He said, in part:

> *It is with no wish to cast reproach upon the respectable Society of Friends that the fact is recorded that at the commencement of the differences between the American colonists and the home Government, and until the event of war settled the points at issue in favor of the cause of freedom, the sympathies of those who controlled the public action of that Society were with the Crown. The leading members of that Society were men who had grown old in the habit of loyalty, and had been rewarded therefore by dignities and wealth. Their government of the colony had always been peaceful, the spirit of resistance threatened war, and war was not only a subversion of their religious principles, but it threatened ruin to their worldly fortunes. With the habitual caution of men advanced in years, they looked with disfavor on the hot-headed young patriots who declared themselves supporters of so radical a change as the establishment of an independent government.*

Calling together the first Continental Congress was an act of heroic patriotism from the American standpoint, but was mere treasonable plotting in the royalists' eyes. In 1774, the General Yearly Meeting of Friends warned members of all Meetings not to depart from their peaceful principles by taking part in any of the political matters then being stirred up, reminding all Friends that under the King's government they had been favored with a peaceful and prosperous enjoyment of their rights, and strongly suggesting the propriety of disowning all such members as disobeyed the orders issued by the Yearly Meeting.

However, many younger members took an active part in supporting the Continental Congress and the armies. They had to resist the prejudices which they had been educated in and by which they were surrounded. They gladly gave to the cause out of their purses and stocks of goods. They took the oath of allegiance to the governing body in Pennsylvania when required to do so, and accepted being read out of Meeting.

Quoting Charles Wetherill further:

On one other point they [Free Quakers] differed radically from the older Society, and that was as to the right of offering forcible resistance against warlike invasion. The Quakers had always held that resistance was sinful, and so they adhered to an absolute peace, under all circumstances, suffering violence to themselves, their families, and their country rather than offer any resistance or serve in the army, even going so far as to refuse to pay taxes where the money was being raised for military purposes. The Free Quakers held, admitting the necessity of government, that all government is essentially a defensive war [a curious expression] for the protection of public peace, and that when the government is threatened by domestic treason or foreign invasion, it then becomes the plain duty of every man to join in the public defense by all means possible, and that war, while an extreme measure, is in such instances not merely justifiable, but right and proper, and, as is shown above, the founders of the Society showed their sincerity in this matter by serving their country, with their very best exertions, at the time of its utmost need. On the same ground they held, contrary to the discipline of Friends, that a man might forcibly resist any bodily violence offered to himself or to any one to whom he owed the duty of protection. While their views as to warfare and resistance were precisely the same as that of nearly all Christians, they were in such striking contrast to the well-settled doctrines of the Friends that they were commonly known, and are still sometimes spoken of, as "fighting Quakers."

Betsy had been disowned by her family's Meeting when she married John Ross, but the Society of Free Quakers, which she joined in 1785, appears to have been very supportive. Numerous entries in the financial records of the Meeting reflect approval of funds to support Betsy and her family through the years. This assistance begins in 1812 when Clarissa Sidney [Exhibit 30], her first child by John Claypoole, was widowed and moved into the Claypoole household with five children. Betsy was sixty years old at this time. Clarissa's sixth child Rachel was born in Betsy's house on June 16, 1812 and in her own words later in life she *"was raised under the care of Betsy."*

It is also at about this time that Betsy was burdened with taking care of her husband John Claypoole who was bedridden as a result of the wounds he received at the Battle of Germantown when the British were occupying Philadelphia. The ledger pages of the Society of Free Quakers show that both Betsy and Clarissa received occasional financial support from the Meeting.

The ledger page beginning with June 1812 (Exhibit 18) has on it the following entry of September 20: to E. Claypoole for boarding J. Claypoole, $72.00. The next entry is a payment to Clarissa Willson [*sic*] $40.00 without comment. A few lines further down we find an entry for shoes for J. Claypoole, $2.25. The next entry is on February 9, 1813, for $46.00 to Elizabeth Claypoole for boarding John Claypoole. Further down on the same page is an entry of $23.00 to C. Willson [*sic*]. On October 7, 1813, there is an entry of $32.00 to E. Claypoole for boarding J. Claypoole and $16.00 to C. Willson [*sic*] without other explanation.

On December 28, 1813 Betsy is paid $33.32 for making cushions for the Meeting House. The next entries regarding the care of J. Claypoole are in 1817, with an entry on April 10 of $26 to Betsy and $13 to Clarissa, followed by a similar entry on July 13, and another on October 10 in the amount of $28.50 to Betsy and $30 to Clarissa. There is one entry in 1818 for Betsy, $26 and Clarissa $13 without explanation. (John Claypoole had died August 3, 1817.)

In 1819 Betsy and Clarissa are paid (twice) for cleaning the meeting house, and in 1820, 1822, 1823, 1824 and 1825 Clarissa receives money for the schooling of her children.

While it is clear that the Meeting felt Betsy and her extended family needed a little financial help, she was not the only recipient of the generosity of the Society of Free Quakers. The records indicate at least one other person was being given financial support for "boarding." In many other instances through the years, small gifts were made to individuals who were unnamed except as being "a poor woman." Also, the costs of burial of the very young were often covered by the Meeting.

The Philadelphia *Inquirer* column reports, "*William H. Wetherill, our veteran white lead manufacturer, who is now nearing ninety himself, has told me that his father and Betsy Ross were the last to attend a meeting of the Free Quakers in religious worship. For a long time the attendance at Meeting was confined to a very few persons. On that last day the flag maker, a very old lady, and John Price Wetherill were alone. And when leaving the old structure at Fifth and Arch, he turned the key, it closed forever the Free Quaker*

Meeting House as a place of worship." [The Society of Free Quakers exists today as a philanthropic organization.]

The Pennsylvanian, a daily newspaper in Philadelphia, carried an obituary notice on Tuesday, February 2, 1836, saying that Elizabeth Claypoole passed away in the afternoon January 30th, age 84. [She was at the home of her daughter Jane Canby in Philadelphia.] There were eleven other death notices published that day of gentlemen, ladies, and infants, including in some instances comment as to the nature of the illness, or an open invitation to attend the funeral. The paper published whatever it was given. Nothing noteworthy about Betsy was brought forward by the person who gave the death notice to the paper.

Chapter 7

Canby's Speech before the Historical Society of Pennsylvania

*I*t was in late May or early June of 1776, according to the speech given by William Canby, that Betsy was visited with regard to making a flag by a 'committee' of three men, being her late husband's uncle George Ross, a Colonel in the Pennsylvania militia; Robert Morris, the Quaker financier whose private fortune later helped save the American Revolution; and George Washington. Her participation in the design of the flag, and her contribution of the five-pointed star, is the Betsy Ross story originally told by William J. Canby.

Canby, in the part of his speech devoted to the business of Betsy and the 'committee', has this to say:

> *After the death of her husband, being without any means to depend upon but her hands, she rented the little house we have described, and "hung up her shingle", inviting her former customers to her shop. With all her patient industry and perseverance, however, she found it difficult to get along, as the "hard times" brought about by the revolutionary war came upon her. She often pondered over the future, and brooded sometimes almost to despondency upon her troubles, yet she always rallied when she reflected upon the goodness of Providence who had never deserted her.*

> *Sitting sewing in her shop one day with her girls around her, several gentlemen entered. She recognized one of these as the uncle of her deceased husband, Colonel George Ross, a delegate from Pennsylvania to Congress. She also knew the handsome form and features of the dignified, yet graceful and polite Commander in Chief, who, while he was yet Colonel George Washington had visited her shop both professionally and socially many times, (a friendship caused by her connection with the Ross family). They announced themselves as a committee of congress, and stated that they had been appointed to prepare a flag, and asked her if she thought she*

could make one, to which she replied, with her usual modesty and self reliance, that "she did not know but she could try; she had never made one but if the pattern were shown to her she had not doubt of her ability to do it." The committee was shown into her back parlor, the room back of the shop, and Colonel Ross produced a drawing, roughly made, of the proposed flag. It was defective to the clever eye of Mrs. Ross and unsymmetrical, and she offered suggestions which Washington and the committee readily approved.

What all these suggestions were we cannot definitely determine, but they were of sufficient importance to involve an alteration and re-drawing of the design, which was then and there done by General George Washington, in pencil, in her back parlor. One of the alterations had reference to the shape of the stars. In the drawing they were made with six points. Mrs. Ross at once said that this was wrong; the stars should be five pointed; they were aware of that, but thought there would be some difficulty in making a five pointed star. "Nothing easier" was her prompt reply and folding a piece of paper in the proper manner, with one clip of her ready scissors she quickly displayed to their astonished vision the five pointed star (Exhibit 3) which accordingly took its place in the national standard. General Washington was the active one in making the design, the others having little or nothing to do with it. When it was completed, it was given to William Barrett, painter, to paint.

He had no part in the design, he only did the painting. (He was a first-rate artist. He lived in a large three story brick house on the East side of an alley which ran back to the Pennsylvania Academy for young ladies, which was kept by James A. Neal; said to be the best institution of the kind at that time in Philadelphia. The house is yet standing. [1870])

The committee suggested Mrs. Ross to call at a certain hour at the counting house of one of their number, a shipping merchant, on the wharf. Mrs. Ross was punctual to the appointment. The gentleman drew out of a chest an old ship's color, which he loaned her to show her how the sewing was done, and also the drawing painted by Barrett. Other designs had been prepared by the committee and one or two of them were placed in the hands of other seamstresses to be made. Betsy Ross went diligently to work upon her flag, carefully examining the peculiar stitch in the old ship's color, which had been given her as a specimen, and recognizing, with the eye of a good mechanic its important characteristics, strength and elasticity.

The flag was soon finished, and Betsy returned it, the first 'Star Spangled Banner' that ever floated upon the breeze, to her employer. It was run up to the peak of one of his ships lying at the wharf, and received the unanimous approval of the committee and of a little group of bystanders looking on, and the same day was carried into the State House and laid before Congress, with a report from the committee.

The next day Col. Ross called upon Betsy, and informed her that her work had been approved and her flag adopted; and he now requested her to turn her whole attention to the manufacture of flags, and gave her an unlimited order for as many as she could make; desiring her to go out forthwith and buy all the "bunting and tack" in the city, and make flags as fast as possible. Here was astounding news to Betsy! Her largest ideas of business heretofore had been confined to the furnishing of one or two houses at a time with beds, curtains and carpets; and she had only recently been depressed with the prospect of losing much of this limited business by reason of the high prices of materials, and the consequent retrenchment by citizens in luxuries that could be dispensed with.

She sat ruminating upon her sudden good fortune some minutes before it occurred to her that she had not the means to make the extensive purchases required by the order; and, therefore, she would be utterly helpless to fill it; for these were the days of cash transactions, and such a thing as a poor person getting credit for a large amount of goods was altogether unheard of. Here was a dilemma. What was she to do? Like many others, she began already to doubt her good fortune and to dash her rising hopes with the reflections, "this is too good luck for me, it cannot be". Rising superior to this, however, she said to herself, "We are not creatures of luck: Have I not found that the Good One has never deserted me, and He will not now. I will buy all the bunting I can, and make it into these flags, and will explain to Mr. Ross why I cannot get anymore. He will, no doubt, give orders to others, and so I shall lose a large part of this business: But I must be satisfied with a moderate share of it, and grateful too." So she went to work. Scarcely had she finished her cogitations when Col. Ross re-entered the shop. "It was very thoughtless of me" he remarked, "when I was just here now, that I did not offer to supply you with the means for making these purchases; it might inconvenience you" he said delicately, "to pay out so much cash at once, here is something to begin with" (giving her a one hundred pound note) and you must draw on me at sight for what ever you require."

According to Canby, Mrs. Ross was now effectively set up in the business of flag and color making for the government; through all her later life, which was a long, useful, and eventful one, she *"never knew what it was"* to use her own expression, *"to want employment."* This business (flag making for the government) remained with her and in her family business for many years.

In Canby's speech, and in the later testimonies as to what Betsy said, we have it that General Washington was the active one in presenting the initial drawing of a flag, and in drawing the revised design for the flag to incorporate Betsy's suggestions. (These had to do with a change in the dimensions of the flag, the use of five-pointed stars, and the thought that the stars should be arranged in some symmetrical fashion.) After Washington redrew the flag, incorporating her suggestions, a painting was made from the drawing and the flag was produced.

This view of what transpired when the 'committee' brought a flag design to Betsy is consistent with the adoption by the Marine Committee of the circle of stars flag design a year later for the Continental Navy. However, while this flag had more visual and symbolic appeal than other designs, it was not an easy flag to make and it did not come into general use. Its design was principally used by artists throughout the years to represent the flag of the new nation.

Canby's report of Betsy making a flag for Washington is confirmed (discussed later) by Rebecca Sherman, wife of Roger Sherman of Connecticut. While the design of the flag is not known, it was always believed to have been the circle-of-stars flag. The family tradition is represented in the early art.

The mistake that has been made was to assume only one flag design emerged from this period, that it was the one made by Betsy Ross to conform to Washington's drawing, and that this was the one later adopted by the Marine Committee for the Navy. Neither William Canby nor George Canby was ever able to establish that as fact. Two flags evolved, one designed by George Washington, which Betsy made, and one by person or persons unknown used by the Pennsylvania Navy.

Chapter 8

The Artistic Record

The early existence of folklore and art gives strong support to the family story as told by William Canby in 1870. However, there is no clear record, only supposition, as to who proposed the "new constellation" (circle of stars) flag approved by the Marine Committee for the Navy. Schuyler Hamilton was unable to find an answer to that question in the official records of the time, so it could follow that it came to be attributed to the 'committee' and the person they chose to make the flag, Betsy Ross.

When Betsy was selected to make a flag, we know without doubt that she was well known to important people, at least in the city of Philadelphia. It is reasonable to assume, because of her involvement with making early flags, that she became something of a celebrity, and towards the end of her life, the subject of several paintings.

The fact Betsy was paid by the State Navy Board for 'colours' delivered to Captain Richards brought her work to the attention of important men besides Robert Morris and Colonel George Ross. According to Canby/Balderston (1909) the following were members of the Board that authorized the payment by William Webb: William Bradford, Joseph Marsh, Joseph Blewer, and Paul Cox. This would add to the number of men in Philadelphia who knew from a very early date of the role of the "Little Rebel" upholsterer in Philadelphia in making our first naval flag.

Ellie Wheeler

A significant painting was done in 1851, by an amateur artist named Ellie Wheeler, a daughter of well-known artist Thomas Sully and wife of Philadelphia attorney John Hill Wheeler (Exhibit 6). It depicts Betsy Ross with three men and a child in attendance, and a flag on her lap with five-pointed stars in a circle. Owned by Weston Adams, the picture predates by almost 20 years the speech by William Canby, and by forty years the picture by Charles H. Weisgerber, *"Birth of Our Nation's Flag"*

Weston Adams, (1988) who is descended from Sarah Griscom, Betsy's older sister, dealt with the question of Betsy's celebrity in his publication *Art as Evidence in The Betsy Ross Story*. He writes that *"her late husband was well connected."* John Ross had *"two uncles who signed the Declaration of Independence, George Read and George Ross (who was also an aide to General Washington), and another uncle, Edward Biddle, who was a member of the Continental Congress."* Adams feels this made her a likely choice of the committee.

According to Adams (1988) *"The artist Ellie Wheeler grew up in the neighborhood where Betsy Ross lived and was twenty years old when Betsy died in 1836. It can be safely assumed that the young artist was aware that her elderly neighbor was known in her time for the historical event shown in the painting."* Adams is suggesting that the story of the 'committee' and Betsy's role as flag maker was common knowledge in Philadelphia while she was alive, and that as folklore after her death it was generally assumed the 'new constellation' flag was made by her.

Weston Adams interprets the 1851 Wheeler painting showing Betsy with the 'committee' as a painting of a 'celebration' with Betsy presenting our nation's first flag to the men who first envisioned it. Folklore would appear to have confirmed the Marine Committee flag as the one the 'committee' approved a year earlier.

I am indebted to Weston Adams for his research and publication of *Art as Evidence in the Betsy Ross Story*. The image reproduced as Exhibit 6 is of the original painting in his possession, a painting by Ellie Wheeler. However, a similar painting by J. L. G. Ferris (1863-1930), titled *Betsy Ross and the Flag Committee* is more widely known. This painting (Exhibit 7) was widely reproduced and sold in competition with the Weisgerber painting, but there is no question where Ferris got his inspiration. It was one of seventy paintings he did for his series *The Pageant of a Nation*. In 1917 a special gallery was built in the Museum of Independence Hall to house this collection. The paintings were bequeathed to the Smithsonian Institute by Ferris after his death in 1930. These were de-accessioned by the Smithsonian and returned to the family in the late 1970s.

There is a painting done by James Peale in 1805 identified as *Elizabeth Claypoole* by the brass plate on the front, in the records of the Pennsylvania Academy of Fine Arts, and in lists of Peale's works. It was donated in 1939 as part of a collection by Mrs. John Frederick Lewis. In his publication, Adams questions how such a fine painting by a well-established artist could be Elizabeth (Betsy Ross) Claypoole, yet if it were true, it would be consistent with his theory that the recognition she enjoyed in her lifetime made her an important figure and justified this portrait. As it turns out, it is a matter of mistaken identity.

The person James Peale painted is the daughter of James and Mary Claypoole born 17 May 1751 and died 5 April 1829. This Elizabeth Claypoole married (1) Captain Morris Copper on 19 November 1774 and (2) Colonel Timothy Matlack on 17 August 1797, her first husband having been lost at sea during the Revolutionary War. The Pennsylvania Academy of Fine Arts has advised that on the back of the picture it states the subject is Elizabeth Claypoole Matlack, and that the name on the brass plate on the front of the picture is incomplete.

Samuel L. Waldo

A portrait painted in 1832 by the famed artist Samuel L. Waldo provides evidence that Betsy, in her lifetime, was seen as a significant person. The existence of this painting was brought to light by Whitney Smith, Ph.D. (1975), a noted flag expert. Smith wrote that the painting was signed on the back by the artist along with the name of the subject as "Betsy Ross" and the date 1832. The portrait is a reasonable likeness of Betsy as can be confirmed by a comparison with photographs of two of her female descendants (Exhibits 1 & 2, and Exhibits 29 a & b).

Smith published a photograph of the picture, having been encouraged by the owner to make its existence public, to describe how it was discovered, and to report the signature on the back was confirmed as that of the artist. Smith surmised that Waldo, a well known New York portrait painter who often traveled to Philadelphia on commissions, apparently took the time to look up Elizabeth Claypoole and paint her.

Dr. Smith may not have been totally convinced of the validity of Betsy's story but he appears to regard the painting as genuine. The current owner, who wishes to remain anonymous, has again validated the signature of the artist against known signatures. The image and the writing on the back of the canvas are reproduced by permission of the current owner (Exhibits 1 & 2). Elizabeth Claypoole would have been 80 years old at the time the portrait was painted, living in Abington, Pennsylvania, with a daughter. We can only speculate as to the folklore that prompted this New York artist who, with business in Philadelphia, searched her out to do the painting and then apparently kept it in his portfolio.

An Unknown Artist

A second image of Betsy, apparently done in her lifetime, is referenced by Weston Adams and appears in the book *Betsy Ross, the Griscom Legacy* by Timmins and Yarrington (1983). The picture is held by the Free Library of Philadelphia (Exhibit 28). The artist is unknown, but according to Timmins the flag on her lap would have twenty-four stars, if fully visible, which would date the painting to c. 1831-1835. This would have meant she was an old woman at the time of the painting, but the artist has portrayed her as being much younger. Timmins states the painting was used widely in advertising after William Canby's speech in 1870 and it is seen in the window of an 1876 picture of the Flag House (Exhibit 21). It should be regarded as difficult to authenticate.

In the early 20th century, George Canby, in writing of the life of Betsy in the *Genealogy of the Claypoole Family*, had this to say: *"It is also to be regretted that, except to the writer's mental vision and to the very few of her grandchildren now living who remember her, no semblance of her personality exists. A picture which has been repeatedly placed before the public and is being constantly reproduced in newspapers and other publications is altogether a most ridiculous and absurd pretense."* The Canbys were unaware of any painting of Betsy.

Draft of Frescoes

There is one more artistic suggestion that folklore existed as late as the 1850s regarding the source of our national flag (Exhibit 16). A glass photographic negative in the possession of the Curator, Office of The Architect of the Capitol, depicts sketches done in 1856 by an architectural draftsman for the consideration of Constantino Brunidi. Brunidi was an Italian artist on the payroll of the Capitol Building who completed a number of frescoes in the building. This proposal was for the Ladies Waiting Room, to depict women who played significant roles in the Revolution. There are four rough illustrations, but no names are attached.

One of the proposed frescoes is a flat panel with a woman [Betsy Ross?] presenting a flag to three men, [the committee?] with more uniformed men in the background. A more typical image, as seen on regimental flags, has a female figure (Liberty) presenting a flag to a single soldier, not to a group. This image could represent the Betsy Ross story.

There are three other rough images intended to fill sections in the ceiling panel and a fourth blank panel. These images are rough and are not reproduced here.

The first section has what appears to be the barrel of a cannon in the drawing. We can surmise from this that it represents Molly Pitcher (Mary Hays McCauly), who manned her husband's cannon at the Battle of Monmouth. She earned the nickname Molly Pitcher for bringing water to wounded on the battlefield. She was honored by Washington after the battle.

The second section of the ceiling panel could represent Lydia Barrington Darragh, the Philadelphia Quakeress who overheard the British Officers billeted in her home planning an attack on Washington at Valley Forge. The next day she obtained a pass to cross the lines on the pretext of obtaining flour in Frankford (which was outside of Philadelphia) and was able to pass word of the impending attack to Washington.

The third part of the ceiling panel might have represented Deborah Sampson who impersonated a man and enlisted in the Continental Army. She served from May 1782 until October 1783 when a medical officer discovered she was a woman and she was honorably discharged by General Henry Knox. Her service was recognized by a lump sum pension from the state of Massachusetts, and in later years by a pension from Congress. Possibly because no drawing existed for the fourth ceiling panel, the project never came to fruition.

Charles Willson Peale (1741-1827) and Princeton

Charles Willson Peale was with Washington's army at the battles of Trenton and Princeton in January 1777. He served as a lieutenant in the American forces under General Cadwalader. While not directly involved in the engagement with the British at Princeton, he nevertheless produced two very significant paintings of Washington having to do with the battle.

The following account of the first significant painting by him is drawn from *The Princeton University Library Chronicle, Vol XIII, No. 4, 1952* written by Donald Drew Egbert, class of 1924.

In January 1779 the Executive Council of Pennsylvania requested Washington to pose for a portrait by Peale and he agreed to do so.

To assure accuracy in the background scene of the portrait, the artist made a trip to Princeton in February 1779. There he made sketches of the battleground terrain and buildings, including Nassau Hall. The painting is generally known as *Washington at Princeton*, but more accurately it is *Washington after the Battle of Princeton* (Exhibit 8).

In the painting, *"Washington appears with his right hand on hip, standing with his left hand resting on the barrel of a fieldpiece beside which are battle flags captured at Trenton and Princeton. In the distant background is Nassau Hall, where the British formally surrendered, and before it marching British prisoners."* Above Washington's head is his headquarters banner with thirteen six-pointed stars in a circle on a blue field. He wears a blue sash across his chest as the badge of the commander-in-chief. There are no stars on the epaulets.

The original of the picture is owned by the Pennsylvania Academy of Fine Arts. The portrait was so popular that many copies of it were ordered, including some sent to Europe. Peale varied details and background with each repetition. Sellers (1969) says that the order of the pictures can be determined by the changes in military insignia, since Peale was alert to general orders on this point and eager to keep each picture up to date. The blue ribbon disappears, replace by rosettes on the epaulettes and these by silver stars that have continued to our time. An excellent example of this series of paintings has been owned by Princeton University since 1924 and hangs in the anteroom of Proctor Hall at the Graduate College.

The origin of the second painting by C. W. Peale, *Washington at the Battle of Princeton* and Washington's relationship with the College of New Jersey (as it was known then) is detailed in *Princeton Portraits*, by Donald Drew Egbert, with the assistance of Diane Martindell Lee, Princeton University Press, Princeton New Jersey, 1947.

The second painting (Exhibit 9) by C. W. Peale was commissioned by the Trustees of Princeton University (then known as the College of New Jersey) on September 24, 1783. Washington had attended the commencement exercises of the class of 1783 in September of that year and the trustees appointed a committee *"to wait on his Excellency to request him to sit for his picture to be taken by Mr. Charles Willson Peale of Philadelphia."* This was done, and the next day General Washington had fifty guineas delivered to the board to accept as a testimony of his respect for the college. The same committee that solicited Washington's picture, acknowledged his gift which presumably paid for the picture. The painting was duly delivered in September 1784 and hung in the college Hall, in an old frame that had held a portrait of George II. The painting is titled *Washington at the Battle of Princeton*, but is often called *The Death of General Mercer,* who suffered mortal bayonet wounds at the hands of the British.

Based upon travel dates, Washington would likely have sat for the portrait between December 8 and 13, 1783, in Philadelphia. In the painting, Washington stands in the foreground with sword uplifted, dressed in the uniform of commander-in-chief, though without the blue ribbon across his chest that formerly denoted his rank. Instead, on his shoulder are epaulets with five-pointed stars (Exhibit 10). At Washington's feet lies General Hugh Mercer, mortally wounded. Two other large figures in the painting are a standard bearer and a man who appears to be an attending physician (possibly Dr. Benjamin Rush who was with Washington's army). General Mercer died nine days after the battle.

In the background, Washington's blue headquarters banner is seen on the field of battle (Exhibit 11). The flag held over his head by the standard bearer has red and white stripes and a blue canton with several five-pointed stars visible in what would have been a circle (Exhibit 10).

There was some artistic license taken with the painting. The figure representing General Mercer is actually his third son, William Mercer, who was an apprentice to C. W. Peale at the time. The face is that of a young man; no effort was made to age the image. We also know that the circle of stars flag was not in general use at the time the painting was done. That he chose to include the flag in this painting suggests it was with Washington at Princeton in January 1777 and that Peale saw it there, although I must acknowledge its presence in the painting could have been symbolic, representing the nation that was coming into existence.

What is particularly intriguing about this painting is that we don't know if Washington knew the flag was in the painting, or was to be part of it, when he posed for it. When the painting was accepted by the board of trustees on September 30, 1784 and hung in the Hall of the college, nobody took exception to the flag image. Washington had the opportunity to see the finished painting when he came to Princeton again five and a half years later, on April 21, 1789. He was on his way to New York to take the oath as president of the United States. He was received at Princeton with the usual address of welcome and congratulation from the College and the town. He apparently spent the night at the home of President Witherspoon.

A reasonable man would certainly believe he was shown the Peale painting hanging in the Hall of the college, and if he had reason to question its accuracy, he would have done so.

Peale's painting was begun in December 1783, only a few years after the Flag Resolution was passed. I believe the design was Washington's, that it was made by Betsy, and these facts were known to a number of people at the time the Marine Committee adopted the "new constellation" flag on June 14, 1777. Betsy became well-established as a flag maker in those years and this was the beginning of the folklore that attached to her in later years. Peale's painting, admired by many, helped establish the circle of stars design as our symbolic flag. [In considering these arguments, please read Chapter 11, Corroborating Evidence.]

Washington apparently did not have this flag with him on Long Island as there is a British report of the Grand Union flag being flown there. If he had this flag at Trenton and Princeton, it could have reached him after his return with his demoralized troops to the Pennsylvania side of the Delaware River in early December 1776 after his defeats in New York. According to Fischer (2003), Washington asked his men whose enlistments were up as of December 31, 1776, to stay with him for one more month, promising hard currency payment of $10. To obtain the necessary funds, he wrote Robert Morris in Philadelphia who solicited the needed money and sent it on. The flag could have come from Philadelphia with that money. Whether or not the flag was with Washington at Trenton and Princeton is less important than the fact that a flag of that design was in existence.

Emanuel Leutze

It is also worth noting that another artist painted Washington with a circle of stars flag when his army was crossing the Delaware to attack the Hessians at Trenton. Emanuel Leutze, born in Germany but brought to Philadelphia as a child, grew up in the town in the 1820s and 30s before his family relocated to Fredericksburg, Virginia. He would have learned about the flag flown at Trenton and Princeton from the folklore in the town, and when he returned to Germany to study art he took that memory with him. The result was the famous painting, done in Germany in 1851 (which would have been the 75th anniversary of the beginning of the American Revolution), known as *Washington Crossing the Delaware*. He incorporated a circle of stars flag in the painting.

Admiral Furlong (1981) states unequivocally that the flag in the picture is the wrong one, as it did not exist prior to its adoption by the Marine Committee in June of 1777. (It may not have been official, but indications are that it was under consideration.) Furlong would have had Leutze use the Grand Union Flag. But what Leutze did is consistent with Peale's picture, so the origin of the Betsy Ross legend is based on her work of 1776-1777.

Chapter 9

Betsy's Star Spangled Banner

*A*s previously discussed, it is almost a century after the date of the 'committee' calling on Betsy that the general public is made aware in 1870 of the family story when a grandson, William J. Canby (born August 1, 1825) tells it to the Historical Society of Pennsylvania. He relates how, when he was eleven, he was present when his grandmother described to her grandchildren how she made the first *"Star Spangled Banner"* for George Washington, Robert Morris, and her uncle-in-law George Ross. In her recall, she believed that when the three men called on her to discuss having her make a flag, they were a Committee of Congress and that George Washington was in charge. William Canby later calculated the likely date for this meeting to have been about a month before the signing of the Declaration of Independence, a point in time when Washington was in Philadelphia. Betsy would have been a widow for about five months.

Although William Canby first heard the story when he was eleven, he did not investigate it until years later. It was brought to mind when Betsy's first born, Clarissa Sidney Wilson (commonly called Clara), dictated her memoirs to him in the late 1850s. Clarissa had married Jacob Wilson, a merchant trader, who died in 1812. After his death, Clarissa moved from Baltimore to give birth to her sixth child, Rachel, and live with her mother. Clarissa was admitted to membership in the Society of Free Quakers July 6th, 1832. Clarissa also reportedly worked with her mother in the upholstery shop.

Clarissa Sidney (Claypoole) Wilson passed away on July 10, 1863 at her daughter Susan Seller's home in Fort Madison, Iowa. Sellers wrote her Aunt Jane as follows [in part]:

She left us at noon yesterday falling to sleep so calmly and peacefully that we did not know at what moment the Spirit took its flight. She was confined to her room less than two weeks, only a few days of which she was confined to bed. We were more fearful she would suffer greatly at the last, but I am thankful to say she did not appear to do so. Her only care seemed to be a fear of giving trouble to those around her. For herself she seemed to have but little thought except that she might be patiently waiting when the Summons came, and truly we can't doubt that it found her ready.

In Canby's speech, Betsy is said to have described how a drawing of a flag was shown to her, how she suggested some changes in dimensions as well as the use of a five-pointed star instead of one with six points, and how she made a sample flag that was run up to the mast-head of a merchant ship lying at or near the Race Street wharf, and was cheered by those who saw it. She later was told by Colonel Ross that the flag had been accepted and that she should collect materials and begin making flags of that design. The record shows she was paid in late May 1777, prior to the passage of the Flag Resolution, for supplying colours (flags) to the storekeeper of the Pennsylvania Navy.

Before giving his speech, Canby undoubtedly talked with the others who had heard the story. He spent considerable time trying to find confirmation of this story in government records, without success, except for the payment to Betsy for flags delivered to the Pennsylvania Navy. After Canby gave his 1870 speech, he obtained testimonials from three elderly ladies who had worked with Betsy in their earlier years. These ladies confirm the story that Canby told, with a few variations in detail, supporting its credibility. Historians, however, generally regard the account of the making of the first flag as essentially hearsay without any basis in fact, and challenge it because important specifics cannot be corroborated. However, we now believe that we have independent corroboration of the essence of the story, and that there is strong circumstantial evidence that a flag was made for Washington, but not for the army or navy at this time. This is consistent with the fact that Washington, in his various letters to the Board of War concerning a flag for the Army, never mentions meeting with Betsy.

Further, there is an absence of any record of a Committee of Congress (although it could have been an informal, secret committee) having been appointed for the purpose of having a flag made, or of having approved a flag. If in fact the Continental Congress was not involved and the flag was made personally for Washington, the flag for the Pennsylvania Navy would have come later as a marine flag.

The concept of a national flag did not really catch on in the early years of the Revolution. The separate States were not that United. In 1783, according to Henry Moeller, the Secretary of the Congress, Charles Thomson, had the Flag Resolution republished in various newspapers, perhaps seeking to have the states adopt a single national flag. This would likely have been the circle of stars design adopted June 14, 1777. However, nothing came of this as it was probably too early for the states to adopt and identify with a single national flag. Flags for maritime purposes were another story, with several variations in general use.

One possible reason why the circle of stars flag did not "catch on" except perhaps as a symbolic flag would be the difficulty of making it (dividing the circle into 13 increments) and low visibility at sea. We did not need a national flag and it was not a useful maritime flag. Putting the stars in lines was simpler. *Our Flag* (2001) states that the circle of stars flag did begin to appear in use about 1790, and there is pictorial evidence after that date of flags flying from ships with circular designs in the canton. To some extent, this confirms that the circle of stars flag gained recognition as a national flag, but in conjunction with other star alignments.

Stars and stripes flags used in the 1780s and 1790s by the army are described by Furlong and McCandless. When the British did not withdraw from the northwest in accordance with the treaty that ended the war, the government, under the Articles of Confederation, raised a small army and built two forts to protect the settlers in the frontier area: Fort Harmer on the Muskingham River and Fort Washington near present-day Cincinnati. Drawings exist that show the flags which were in use, the Fort Harmer drawing shows five-pointed stars in lines, the Fort Washington drawing is unclear as to the points on the stars, but they are arranged in lines (on a diagonal to fit into the small space on the drawing).

If the circle of stars flag were in use, it may have flown on July 4, 1788, in Philadelphia. The adoption of the Constitution was celebrated with a "Grand Procession," organized by Francis Hopkinson who was the Grand Marshall and who participated as a Judge of the Admiralty. He described the event in great detail in notes that were published after his death. He reports that a Captain Bell carried the **Flag of the United States** (emphasis added). When Washington took the oath of office in New York in 1789 as first president, it is reported that the United States flag was raised to the cupola of the building as a signal for a thirteen gun salute. Whatever the flag was, a national flag was recognized.

As to Betsy's work, it would appear that she made flags to order, in whatever design was required. Howard Madaus, in his study *The United States Flag in the American West* (1998), identifies Elizabeth Claypoole as making flags for the Indian Bureau in the period between 1810 and 1820. He also mentions a William Barrett as being a painter of eagles on flags for use as gifts to Indian tribes. This is likely the same Barrett who did the watercolor of the design Betsy proposed to the committee, and Betsy would have worked with him many times in making flags that required painted images.

Betsy had recommended using a five-pointed star, and we can infer from the 1784 painting by Charles Willson Peale, (Exhibit 9) executed for the College of New Jersey and entitled *Washington at the Battle of Princeton*, that a circle of stars flag existed at the time of the battle, with five-pointed stars in the blue field of the canton. Peale depicted Washington accurately in the 1784 painting: he has three five-pointed stars on an epaulet on the shoulder of his uniform. He is not wearing the blue sash shown in the earlier paintings to denote his authority. Peale is known as being exacting in his details, and he was at the Battle of Princeton, so it is interesting that he painted the circle of stars flag. In this picture, he has Washington's blue headquarters banner shown on the field of battle behind Washington. His 1779 painting *Washington after the Battle of Princeton* features Washington's Headquarters banner prominently.

The existence of the circle of stars flag, depicted in the 1784 painting, may be confirmed by the story of Captain Williams from the Mexican War, discussed in Chapter 11. He carried a Betsy Ross flag with him, one which people of that day commonly referred to as the *Trenton Flag*.

In all likelihood, the people of Philadelphia and those who worked for Betsy in her shop were well aware that during the early years of the Revolution, Betsy had been actively involved in making flags for the navy, and possibly directly for George

Washington's use (but not the Army flag he was anticipating). Let us assume the public in Philadelphia knew of her flag work but not necessarily the details of how it came to be. Folklore would have taken on a life of its own that would have associated Betsy with the circle of stars flag, whether or not she was directly involved in its creation.

In 1796, Betsy's widowed niece Margaret Boggs and her infant son John moved in with Betsy, and Margaret joined the family flag-making business. In testimony years later, Boggs said that Betsy often related the story of making the flag for Washington. We must assume therefore, that it was common knowledge. In 1812, Betsy's daughter Clarissa and family moved in with Betsy. This would have been thirty-six years after the 'committee's visit', and more than a year before the bombardment of Fort McHenry. As to how Betsy came to describe her flag as the first "star spangled banner," we can only assume that the story took on special meaning after the bombardment of Fort McHenry, which would have given the term "Star Spangled Banner" special significance in her mind. How Betsy's recall would differ from the facts, we can only surmise, but when Betsy told the story later in her life, it probably took on a few modifications typical of oral history.

Washington was a highly revered figure in the country, and Betsy would point out to her grandchildren, as recalled by William Canby, that Washington was *"First in War, First in Peace, and First in the Hearts of His Countrymen."* Betsy is remembered as saying that she *"was more honored by having entertained Washington in her parlor than she was at the making of the first flag."*

Betsy was proud of her work during the early years. She told her grandchildren, according to Canby, that when flags came back to her for repairs she could always tell which she had made and that she had made most of them.

As to the 'committee', she would hardly have been in error in identifying George Washington as one in the group who visited her. It was not Benjamin Franklin, and certainly not Francis Hopkinson as some historical revisionists would have us believe.

William Canby's Research

William Canby made a serious attempt to find evidence of a circle of stars flag being used after the Declaration of Independence and before the Flag Resolution passed, and he reported on two paintings of Washington by artists who represented that the new flag was in use at the battle of Princeton in January 1777. Trumbell was one, but his painting was done much later. The flag he painted in the picture has the stars in a square with one in the middle and is shown in his other paintings. The most convincing picture is by C. W. Peale, painted for the College of New Jersey (Princeton), commissioned by the trustees.

There is the intriguing account of Lieutenant William Digby, who served under General Burgoyne in the ill-fated 1777 campaign to reach Albany and split the colonies. George Canby uncovered this through reading contemporary papers preserved in London, and had been in correspondence with B. F. Stevens and Brown of London in regard to a flag taken in the action around Fort Ticonderoga in early July 1777. A letter from Stevens and Brown to George Canby, dated 21 January 1903, quoting from the Diary of Lt. Wm. Digby (in the possession of the British Museum) describes the military actions and in particular the taking of Fort Ann. He states, *"At that action (on July 8) the 9th regiment took their colours which were intended as a present to their Colonel, Lord Leganeer"* (sic Ligonier). *"They were very handsome, a Flag of the United States, 13 Stripes, alternate red and white, in a blue field representing a new constellation."*

Canby was puzzled that the words "13 stars white" were missing, and wrote Stevens and Brown to confirm the quotation, suspecting that the copyist had inadvertently omitted the words "thirteen stars" in transcribing the quote from the diary. Stevens and Brown confirmed that they had the quotation correct. As a further check on this, a Mr. Smith Burnham, Professor of History at the West Chester State Normal School, who was in London in the fall of 1908, was asked to examine the Diary.

He confirmed the accuracy of the quotation, noting that *"The whole diary seems to be the work of a keen observer, who writes out very clearly what he sees."* Digby was among the British officers who surrendered to General Horatio Gates at Saratoga, October 17th, 1777. The diary was apparently written out after the author returned to England, perhaps six months after the surrender, from a draft or notes taken during the campaign, which may explain why the wording of his description of the flag captured at Fort Ann follows so closely the resolution of Congress, and also how the absence of the reference to "13 stars" could have been a simple oversight.

More Recent Research

While we have this exhaustive investigation into the possible use of a flag based on the specifics of the Flag Resolution, there is evidence the Grand Union flag was still being used well after the Declaration of Independence, and even after the Flag Resolution. When Burgoyne moved south down Lake Champlain in 1777 toward Albany, a second British army under Brigadier General Barry St. Leger moved down from Canada via Lake Ontario, landing near Oswego, and advanced toward Albany via the Mohawk River Valley. The British laid siege to Fort Schuyler (near present-day Rome) but were prevented from taking the fort through the aggressive action of the Americans under General Herkimer, and a clever ruse by Major General Benedict Arnold. General St. Ledger then retreated back to Canada, never providing Burgoyne with the support for which he was looking (Furlong and McCandless, 1981).

Eggenberger (1964) has summed up this episode concisely in his book and describes how the patriots improvised a *"Continental (Grand Union) Flag"* by using red and white "stripes" and blue "strips" cut from garments donated by members of the garrison. There is no mention of stars, and Eggenberger says, *"Undoubtedly the strips were the eight blue triangles which would form the British Union in the Canton." "Corroborating evidence that the Fort Schuyler flag was the Grand Union comes from a carving on a powder horn owned by John McGraw, one of the fort's soldiers in the autumn of 1777. With loving care McGraw carved out a reproduction of the fort showing a flag hoisted above it — the Grand Union — and when finished he inscribed the date "December 25, 1777" — a date that will live longer in history as Christmas Day at Valley Forge."*

Although the use of thirteen red and white stripes was universal at this time, we can conclude from these bits of historical evidence that the image of a national flag with stars on the blue field of the canton was not yet established in the minds of the fighting forces on land, however, marine flags with stars and stripes were already in use and one of those designs evolved into the "Star Spangled Banner."

Chapter 10

The Testimonies

After William Canby had given his speech, he collected testimonies from Rachel Fletcher and two other women who worked for Betsy. He wanted to confirm for historical purposes the family story which he had made public. He wrote to Rear Admiral George Preble (1887) in response to a letter from him concerning the family story that it was "report" and not "supposition." Preble makes no comment on this.

The following three women gave the testimonies; each "affirmed" before a Notary Public. [Quakers do not swear to the truthfulness of something they say because it implies they are not always truthful; instead they affirm the truthfulness of their testimony.]

(1) Margaret Donaldson Boggs: born in 1776 to Betsy's sister Sarah, who was two and a half years older than Betsy. Margaret married Joseph Boggs in 1794 and was widowed in 1796. She had a son, John, and the Meeting gave her $5 towards his education while in his teens, but nothing further is known about him. Margaret was an early member of the Society of Free Quakers and a regular attender.

(2) Sophia Hildebrand: a granddaughter of Betsy; the first child of Clarissa Sidney (Claypoole) Wilson. Sophia was born in 1806 and married Charles Hildebrand (date unknown) and had one child about whom nothing is known. Sophia died in 1891.

(3) Rachel Fletcher: Betsy's daughter, born in 1789 and married to John Fletcher in 1823 (her second marriage). Rachel's testimony is the one most generally quoted. It follows in its entirety.

All three of the ladies, in their testimonies, say that Betsy mentioned having made the first Star Spangled Banner. However, only Rachel's testimony is included here since it provides more detail and the others would be redundant.

Testimony of Rachel Fletcher

I remember having heard my mother, Elizabeth Claypoole, say frequently that she, with her own hands, (while she was the widow of John Ross), made the first Star Spangled Banner that ever was made. I remember to have heard her also say that it was made on the order of a committee, of whom Col. Ross was one, and that Robert Morris was also one of the committee. That General Washington, acting in conference with the committee, called with them at her house. This house was on the north side of Arch Street, a few doors below Third Street, above Bread Street, a two story house, with attic and a dormer window, now standing, the only one of the row left, the old number being 89; it was formerly occupied by Daniel Niles, shoemaker. Mother at first lived in the house next east and when the war came she moved into the house of Daniel Niles. That it was in the month of June, 1776, or shortly before the Declaration of Independence, that the committee called on her. That the member of the committee named Ross was an uncle of her deceased husband. That she was previously well acquainted with Washington and that he had often been in her house in friendly visits, as well as on business. That she had embroidered ruffles for his shirt bosoms, and that it was partly owing to his friendship for her that she was chosen to make the flag. That when the committee (with General Washington) came into her store she showed them into her parlor, back of her store, and one of them asked her if she could make a flag; and that she replied that she did not know, but she could try. That they then showed her a drawing, roughly executed, of the flag as it was proposed to be made by the committee, and that she saw in it some defects in its proportions and in the arrangement and shape of the stars. That she said it was square and that a flag should be one-third longer than its width; that the stars were scattered promiscuously over the field, and she said they should be in lines, or in some adopted form, as a circle or a star, and that the stars were six-pointed in the drawing, and she said they should be five-pointed. That the gentlemen of the committee and General Washington very respectfully considered her suggestions and acted upon them, General Washington seated himself at a table with pencil and paper, altered the drawing to the suggestions of my mother. That

General Washington seemed to her to be the active one in making the design, the others having little or nothing to do with it. That the committee then requested her to call on one of their number, a shipping merchant at the wharf, and then adjourned. That she was punctual to her appointment, and then the gentleman drew out of a chest an old ship's color which he loaned her to show her how the sewing was done, and also gave her the drawing finished to her suggestions. That this drawing was done in water colors by William Barrett, an artist, who lived on the north side of Cherry Street, above Third Street, a large three story brick house on the west side of an alley which ran back to the Pennsylvania Academy for Young Ladies, kept by James Neal, the best school of the kind in the city at that time. That Barrett only did the painting, and had nothing to do with the design. He was often employed by mother afterward to paint coats-of-arms of the United States and of the State on silk flags. That other designs had also been made by the committee and given to other seamstresses to make, but they were not approved. That mother went diligently to work upon her flag and soon finished it, and returned it, the first Star Spangled Banner that ever was made, to her employers; that it was run up to the peak of one of the vessels belonging to one of the committee then lying at the wharf, and was received with shouts of applause by the few bystanders who happened to be looking on. That the committee on the same day carried the flag into the Congress, sitting in the State House, and made a report, presenting the flag with the drawing, and that the next day Colonel Ross called upon my mother and informed her that her work had been approved and her flag adopted; and he gave orders for the purchase of all the materials, and the manufacture of as many flags as she could make. And that from that time forward, for over fifty years, she continued to make flags for the United States Government."

I believe the facts stated in the foregoing article, entitled "The First American Flag, and Who Made It," are all strictly true." [This is an apparent reference to a published version of Canby's speech.]

Signed: Rachel Fletcher

Affirmed and subscribed before Thomas J. McEvily, Notary Public for the City and County of New York, July 31, 1871.

In a footnote to the above, George Canby had this to say:

In this last affidavit, among so many particulars, it is probable that some, at least, are confused, especially in regard to order of time. It is unlikely, for instance, that Mrs. Ross had any familiar acquaintance with Washington before the making of the flag, and if she ever made ruffles for him, it was probably after he came to Philadelphia as President.

Canby also says, "*The short time between the making of the first flag and the issue of unlimited orders for flags seems difficult to accept, in the light of what has been shown.*" "*But taken all together, these [three] affidavits show that Elizabeth Claypoole said that she made the flag about June 1st, 1776, to the order of Washington, Robert Morris, and George Ross; that she suggested the five-pointed star, and that the flag then made afterward became the national standard.*"

While the testimonies given by Boggs, Hildebrand, and Fletcher are the well-known published ones, another testimony exists in the form of a letter written in Fort Madison, Iowa, in 1903 by Clarissa's youngest daughter Rachel when she was 91. The letter is in the possession of the American Flag House and Betsy Ross Memorial in Philadelphia. Rachel was born June 16, 1812 in Betsy's home after her mother was widowed and moved back from Baltimore to live with her mother. In Rachel's own words, she was raised under the care of Betsy. Rachel was thirteen years older than William Canby and it is likely she heard the family story directly from Betsy, confirmed by her mother and her mother's peers in later life. Rachel married Jacob Albright July 22, 1840 and had four children.

The letter Rachel wrote is to a friend, Nellie E. Chaffee, whose girls wanted to know the story of Betsy's life and the making of the first flag. Rachel says in the letter that she is 91 years old, and is the last living granddaughter of Betsy. We can also assume from the tone of the letter that this is not the first time she has told the story, as she suggests she will keep it brief.

After briefly describing Betsy's life and marriage to John Ross, she wrote:

Colonel George Ross, an uncle of her husband's and an officer on General Washington's staff, urged General Washington and the committee that were arranging to have a flag made for the Army to take the design they had drawn to Mrs. Ross, saying she would put it into symmetrical shape for the flag. When the committee with General

Washington called on her and showed her the design, she pointed to the star of six points and said, gentlemen, that is an star of English heraldry, for America it should be five-pointed. An objection was raised that it was difficult to cut correctly a five-pointed star. Mrs. Ross turned to her table took up a piece of paper laid it in folds and with one clip of her scissors opened the paper and placed before them a perfect star which they at once decided to accept.

Toward the end of the letter she wrote:

As Congress had given to her the right to make all the flags for the ships built at the Philadelphia Navy Yard she carried that business on. [Rachel's references to contracts with the Philadelphia Navy Yard could be business that developed in later years. These contracts were certainly not part of the original story of what took place in 1776, and the business continued until 1857.]

Rachel's sister Susan, eighteen months her senior, married Abraham Sellers, and was living in Fort Madison, Iowa when Clarissa Sidney Wilson died there on July 10, 1863. We do not know why Rachel and also Susan were not approached by William Canby to provide a testimony regarding Betsy's story. In all likelihood, he limited his efforts to those women who were locally available to him. He could not have foreseen the need to have more testimonies. At this time, when this letter has just come to light, there is no reason not to accept the testimony of Rachel as being supportive of the others, if not in all the details.

To summarize, the three Quaker ladies, in giving their testimonies, state they heard Betsy say she made the first "Star Spangled Banner." It should be noted that this term was in use before the War of 1812 to describe our national flag but the poem written after the bombardment gave this phrase national prominence. The use of this particular term probably represents one of the ways in which the oral history changed with the passage of time and our interpretation of that oral history would change with intervening events.

Only Margaret Boggs was in the family flag business well before the war of 1812. In her testimony she says Betsy often told the story. Clarissa Wilson moved in with Betsy sometime in 1812, but she could have known the story long before then. Rachel Fletcher would have been about twenty three years old at the beginning of the War of 1812, and might have been in her first marriage. We only know she married John

Fletcher, her second husband, in 1823. Regardless, she is the one who recounts the family story in the most detail in the Testimonies. William Canby says he heard the story first when he was eleven, and Betsy was quite old. But all the testimonies say that Betsy said she made the first "star spangled banner."

Chapter 11

Corroborating Evidence

More evidence supporting the family story has recently come to light from two diverse sources. The first source concerns Rebecca Sherman, who knew Betsy, and the second source relates to Edward Williams, a volunteer in the war with Mexico, and the "Trenton" flag. Both are sources that came to my attention quite propitiously, in the course of conducting research for this book, and both corroborate the family story that Betsy made some important first flags for George Washington.

Rebecca Sherman

We are indebted to Cokie Roberts who, in her book, *Founding Mothers, the Women Who Raised Our Nation (2004)*, quotes the essence of a bit of non-family folklore regarding Betsy Ross. Her source is a 1909 publication, *The Journal of American History*, which recounts the story of Rebecca Sherman.

Rebecca Prescott Sherman (1743-1813) was the first born of Benjamin Prescott and Rebecca Minot, and became the second wife of Roger Sherman of Connecticut, a very important figure in the early affairs of the country, including being a signer of the Declaration of Independence. Her story is given to us by a descendant of her sister, Martha, who was the second child in the family. Martha married Stephen Goodhue. They had a daughter Martha, who is thus a niece of Rebecca Prescott Sherman, and it is the niece from whom we learn the following.

The story of Rebecca's life was told to Mrs. Katherine Prescott (Wright) Bennett (1854-1944), another descendant of Benjamin and Rebecca Minot, who wrote an account of it for publication. Only a portion of this article has to do with Betsy

Ross, the balance being a recounting of various events in the life of Rebecca Prescott Sherman. Mrs. Bennett puts her personal stamp on the Betsy Ross story as follows: *"There is a family tradition, true beyond question. It comes from the best authority as Rebecca Prescott Sherman herself told it to her own niece through whom it came to me."* Mrs. Bennett continues, *"This niece lived to a great age, her faculties unimpaired to the last, her mind clear on all points, especially those connected with her early days."* [A description follows of the elderly lady and her vivid personality and the impression she made on Katherine Prescott Bennett.]

The article provides a description of how Rebecca became the second wife of Roger Sherman just at the time when her beauty, grace and wit were of the greatest help in his career. The niece recalls the elderly aunt as saying, *"We always have been a patriotic race, and this marriage brought Aunt Rebecca into still more active touch with all matters pertaining to the interests of the Colonies at this stirring period; and when at last the Declaration of Independence was declared, can you fancy the excitement and enthusiasm of the wife of Roger Sherman; the man who had so much to do with the momentous document? When a little later George Washington designed and ordered the new flag to be made by Betsy Ross, nothing would satisfy Aunt Rebecca but to go and see it in the works, and there she had the privilege of sewing some of the stars on the very first flag of the young Nation."* The story continues, *"Perhaps because of this experience, she was chosen and requested to make the first flag ever made in the State of Connecticut — which she did, assisted by Mrs. Wooster. This fact is officially recorded."*

No record exists to support the final statement. However, Mrs. Wooster was the daughter of Rev. Thomas Clap, fourth President of Yale, and she was married to Captain David Wooster when he was 35 years old and she was sixteen. During the Revolutionary War, he refused a British commission and served as Commander of the Connecticut troops with the rank of Major-General. He died in April 1777 at Ridgefield, of a wound received in a battle with the British. Mrs. Wooster lived until 1807, much embarrassed in her declining years by her impoverished condition, her husband having used much of his fortune to support the Revolutionary War. Although no record has been found to support Mrs. Wooster's assistance to Betsy in making the first flag made in Connecticut, the Rebecca Prescott Sherman story is entirely consistent with the facts of her existence.

The story, however, is confirmation of a connection between George Washington, Betsy Ross, and our Nation's first flag and it is independent of the descendants of Betsy. Some may think the publication of this story in that era in 1909 could be suspect because of the notoriety attached to the Betsy Ross story, but a shortened version of the article is picked up in 1912 in *Pioneer Mothers of America* by Green and Green. Both publications were extensive histories of the contributions of women in the Revolutionary War period; the flag incident with Rebecca and Betsy was only incidental to the main theme of the two articles.

Another part of the story, as recalled by the niece and told to Mrs. Bennett, had to do with Rebecca and her husband attending a dinner party given by George Washington. The General singled out Rebecca to sit as his side, as being the handsomest lady in attendance that night. The niece related that this did not sit well with Mrs. Hamilton, who was also there. The occasion was significant enough in Rebecca's mind that the dress she wore was cherished and passed down in the family as a keepsake. A piece of the fabric of the dress Rebecca wore that night was given to Katherine Prescott Bennett by the niece, and it was incorporated a bit later as the center piece in a quilt being made by ladies organizing a new chapter of the Daughters of the American Revolution in Minneapolis. That chapter was organized in 1907 as the Rebecca Prescott Sherman Chapter; years later, in 1935, the name was changed to the Fort Snelling Chapter which exists to this day. The significance of this is that the stories out of Rebecca's life as told to Mrs. Bennett by the niece are backed up by material evidence, the piece of the dress in the quilt. Almost a hundred years have gone by, but the quilt survives, in the possession of the Minnesota Historical Society, History Center, known as the Sherman Quilt, accession #65.53.8 (Exhibit 31).

Captain Edward Williams (c. 1819-1900)

A first-hand story of the actions of a volunteer in the War with Mexico provides an independent basis for attributing the Trenton flag, which was re-used during that war, to Betsy. This story first surfaced through the account of an interview with retired General Edward C. Williams, published in the *Harrisburg-Telegraph* on Saturday, February 29, 1896. It is confirmed in all of its specific details by the report of Major William Brindle, Commanding Second Brigade, Volunteer Division, prepared September 15, 1847, the day after the taking of the Mexican Fortress of

Chapultepec on the outskirts of Mexico City. The full report of Major Brindle is Appendix IX in Randy W. Hackenburg's publication *Pennsylvania in The War with Mexico* (1992). The Major describes the assault and in particular the action of Captain E. C. Williams, of Company G "Cameron Guards" of Harrisburg, Pennsylvania. The Major reports that the Captain was struck by a ball, near the top of the shoulder, high enough up to turn the shoulder. Although severely wounded, he was quickly on his feet again, and continued on duty with his company. As the fighting progressed, the Mexican General Bravo surrendered to Captain Williams, and soon thereafter Captain Williams *"ascended to the top of* [the Fortress] *with the first American Flag made by Betsy Ross, of Philadelphia, which was presented to General Washington just before the battle of Trenton, during the Revolution of 1776, which Captain Williams had obtained from the State Library in Harrisburg, Pennsylvania., and carried with him to Mexico, with the purpose of raising it over the enemy's works at every opportunity, and which he raised over the Fortress of Chapultepec at about the same time that a sergeant of one of the old infantry regiments raised a blue regimental flag over it. To Captain Williams belongs the honor of having raised the first American Flag over the Fortress."*

Major Brindle was not alone in knowing that Captain Williams carried an American flag he had "borrowed" from the State Library in Harrisburg. This fact is mentioned by several others in reporting on the action in the Mexican war, reports included in Hackenburg's book.

Going back to the newspaper account from 1896, the newspaper's correspondent writes that *"Captain Williams and Major John Brady borrowed the Trenton flag from James Hoover, State Librarian, in order to decorate a ball room in the old school house on Walnut Street, where the Dauphin Guards then had their armory. This flag was never returned to the State Library."* The flag is described as *"the first American flag ever made, the handiwork of Betsy Ross, and was presented to Gen. George Washington by the maker, just previous to the battle of Trenton, and its authenticity has been known beyond a doubt.... When Captain Williams returned from Mexico he brought with him this historic flag. It was eventually passed to the custodianship of Governor Curtin, was framed, and is now in the possession of Governor Curtin's family."*

The printed account states that it is believed that either Benjamin Rush (1745-1813) or Richard Rush (1780-1859) presented three flags to the State of

Pennsylvania: The old Trenton Flag, the Hessian (a blue flag), and an English flag, These flags were deposited in the State Library in Harrisburg. They could have been given to the State Library while it was in Philadelphia, by Dr. Benjamin Rush, or given to the library when in Harrisburg by Richard Rush. The library in Harrisburg was totally dismantled during the Civil War before the Battle of Gettysburg, when the Confederates were invading Pennsylvania. This could account for the disappearance of all records of the flags. When the Civil War started, Curtin was the Governor and Edward Williams served him and the North in that conflict.

As with the Rebecca Sherman story, this account of Captain Williams' actions could be suspect because of the publicity being given to Betsy Ross's story at about the time of this newspaper account. However, the particulars of this story are part of Major Brindle's report of 1847, filed immediately after the battle, and he specifically mentions the flag and its source. For some reason this report did not become part of the official War Department file (see Appendix 6).

The identification of the American flag as the "Trenton" flag is not unreasonable, especially if it is associated with Dr. Benjamin Rush, best known for promoting inoculation against smallpox. Dr. Rush was present with Washington in the actions at Trenton and Princeton in December 1776 and January 1777 (Fischer 2004). He could have acquired the flags then or been given them later in recognition of the contribution he made in those battles.

Additional, secondary corroborating evidence of Betsy having made a special flag for Washington may be in the coincidence of two painters, Emanuel Leutze and Ellie Wheeler, both showing a circle of stars flag in their work. Emanuel Leutze did his famous *Washington Crossing the Delaware* in 1851, the same year as the Wheeler painting discussed earlier. Both of these artists were young people in Philadelphia in the eighteen twenties and thirties and it would appear that they absorbed folklore that impressed them regarding Betsy having made a special flag for Washington. Thus the image of Betsy that came down thru the years.

Furlong, in *So Proudly We Hail*, is of the opinion regarding Leutze's famous painting that *"The stars and stripes are anachronistic, for they had not yet been adopted at the time of the battle of Princeton."* (i.e. The Flag Resolution was six months later.) Furlong further observes that for Leutze to have been accurate he should have depicted Washington with the Grand Union Flag. Also, historians say he painted the wrong kind of boat, and if in fact Washington had been standing, he might well have fallen overboard. So overall, Leutze's painting is challenged as not being true to life. Regarding Furlong's opinion, being adopted and being in existence are likely two different events.

Chapter 12

Francis Hopkinson – Patriot

We now need to discuss Francis Hopkinson and his possible role in the initial design of our national flag. He is acknowledged to have been a person of considerable talent, a writer, an inventor, poet, artist, and above all, a patriot. Ever since the 1926 biography by George Everett Hastings first brought his name to the fore, a number of historians have grappled with visualizing his flag. While some have developed "conjectural" designs, none of them has considered that Hopkinson's design might not have been adopted and that the flags which became popular were designed by others. A great deal of research fails to provide concrete evidence of a flag designed by Hopkinson having ever been adopted and there is no folklore regarding Hopkinson's claim.

Francis Hopkinson was a well known personality in this period. Although he lived in Bordentown, he had a law practice in Philadelphia and was a member of the American Philosophical Society, which met several times a month. He came from a prominent family. According to the *Dictionary of American Biography* (from which the following is taken), his father, Thomas Hopkinson, a Londoner by birth, was educated at Oxford but came to Philadelphia early in life with his bride, Mary Johnson, daughter of Baldwin Johnson, an Englishman of distinguished family. Thomas Hopkinson held an office in the judiciary under the British Crown in the colony. He was a member of the governor's council, the first President of the American Philosophical Society in Philadelphia, and was a close friend of Benjamin Franklin. Among his contemporaries, he was distinguished for public spirit, good sense, and integrity.

Francis was the oldest of eight children, two of whom died in infancy. He was fourteen when his father died. Francis was the first student to enroll in the Academy of Philadelphia, which opened in 1751, and six years later he received the first diploma granted by the College of Philadelphia. He studied law under Benjamin Chew, and in April 1761 was admitted to the Supreme Court of Pennsylvania. He made a trip to England in 1766 to seek political preferment through the influence of friends and relatives there and visited his mother's cousin, the Bishop of Worcester. He came home after a year abroad but without the appointment he coveted.

He married Ann Borden, daughter of Colonel Joseph Borden, the leading citizen of Bordentown, New Jersey on September 1, 1768. By 1774 he was writing political works concerning the grievances of the colonies. Through the war he served in the Continental Congress in several capacities. His initial appointment was as a member of the Marine Committee on July 12, 1776, and subsequently on November 6, 1776 he was appointed one of three to "execute the business of the navy under the direction of the Marine Committee." [It would have been in this period that he might have conceived the design of a flag to project the image of the developing nation; however no records providing any particular design have been found.]

In the end, Hopkinson made important enemies in the government, which resulted in his resignation from service in the Continental Congress. Nevertheless, he did not lose his interest in politics. In the days of the Constitutional Convention he supported the Federalists and wrote *The New Roof* which was published in the *Pennsylvania Packet* December 29, 1787. In 1790, he was appointed by President Washington to the judgeship of the district court in Pennsylvania, but he had hardly entered upon the office when he died from an attack of apoplexy on May 9, 1791.

Hopkinson's Flag Design, Fact & Fancy

It appears that Hopkinson's claim to having prepared a design for a flag was not seen as important or was simply overlooked in early work on the historical records of the time. In spite of his involvement and influence at the time, the records regarding his claim to having designed our first (national) naval flag were not brought out by biographers until just prior to 1920, long after the Betsy Ross story had taken hold in the country. Schuyler Hamilton, in *The National Flag of the United States* (1852), does not mention either Hopkinson or Betsy Ross but attributes the design of the flag to the Board of War with John Adams as Chairman who *"must have been particularly connected with its preparation."*

The first mention of Francis Hopkinson and his claim to having designed a flag is in the October, 1917, issue of the **National Geographic Magazine**. The *Our Flag* issue is the first publication that reports Hopkinson's claim for compensation in 1780 for the design of a flag he initially refers to as "The Flag of the United States of America" and subsequently as "the great Naval flag of the United States".

The *National Geographic* article identifies the "circle of stars" flag simply as *Flag, June 14, 1777* and calls it, *Our first stars and stripes* (Exhibit 14b), but does not attribute it to anyone. Subsequently, the article observes that "In the navy it became customary to place the stars so as to form the crosses of St. George and St. Andrew" (Exhibit 15b). Apparently the *National Geographic* authors had read what Schuyler Hamilton had to say in his 1887 publication, because the text is so similar, as noted by George Canby in 1909. The result is a naval flag with the stars arranged in the 3-2-3-2-3 order, which is the flag that Congress modified in 1794 with additional stars and stripes.

While the 1917 *National Geographic Magazine* article give no credit to Hopkinson for the June 14, 1777 flag, the publication does detail his claim for compensation for his creative work, and how it is denied.

Immediately after Hopkinson completed his draft design for the Great Seal of the United States, as a consultant to the Second Committee, he wrote a letter to the Board of Admiralty (*National Geographic*, 1917) listing his various artistic labours, modestly looking for acknowledgment and appreciation. George Everett Hastings (1926, pp. 240-241) reports this letter in his *Life and Works of Francis Hopkinson* (following page).

Hopkinson did not ask for monetary compensation, but for some reason he is asked to restate what he has done, and to assign monetary values to his work on the various items.

For our purposes, it is the relative amounts which are most interesting, suggesting his evaluation of the significance, difficulty, or time spent on each (see following Account N° 4). He lists "The Naval Flag of the United States" at 9 pounds, the Seal for the Admiralty (which he was pleased to understand was accepted) at 3 pounds (or one-third that of the value he assigns to the Naval Flag), and the Great Seal at 10

On May 25, 1780, Hopkinson sent to the Board of Admiralty, acting under Congress, the following letter:

GENTLEMEN:

It is with great Pleasure that I understand that my last Device of a Seal for the Board of Admiralty has met with your Honours' Approbation. I have with great Readiness, upon several Occasions exerted my small Abilities in this Way for the public Service; &, as I flatter myself, to the Satisfaction of those I wish'd to please, viz

> The Flag of the United States of America
> 7 Devices for the Continental Currency
> A Seal for the Board of Treasury
> Ornaments, Devices & Checks for the new
>   Bills of Exchange in Spain & Holland
> A Seal for the Ship Papers of the United States
> A Seal for the Board of Admiralty
> The Borders, Ornaments & Checks for the new
>   Continental Currency now in the Press,—a
>   Work of considerable Length
> A Great Seal for the United States of America,
>   with a Reverse.—

For these Services I have as yet made no Charge, nor received any Recompense. I now submit it to your Honours' Consideration, whether a Quarter Cask of the public Wine will not be a proper & a reasonable Reward for these Labours of Fancy and a suitable Encouragement to future Exertions of a like Nature. I sincerely hope your Honours will be of this Opinion and am with great Respect Gentlemen,

> Your Very Humble Servant
> Francis Hopkinson

pounds. The Naval Flag at 9 pounds is nine-tenths as valuable in his eyes as the work he did on the Great Seal.

The implication is that the flag design must be truly an artistic vision. Had his design been accepted, wouldn't he have commented on it in his letter to the Board of Admiralty, or in the invoices he was compiling three years after the date of the Flag Resolution? He simply states as a fact that he prepared a design. This is all that is known about it. It is mentioned in his letter to the Admiralty, and is the first item on his invoices. We do not know the date of that design, he makes no claim that his design was accepted, and there is no record of any acknowledgement to that effect.

"Account N° 4" mentioned in the foregoing report reads as follows:

D⁻ The United States to Francis Hopkinson
    To sundry Drawings & Devices viz⁺

The Naval Flag of the United States.....	£ 9–0–0
Designs with Mottos for Currency.......	7–0–0
Seal of the Board of Treasury...........	3–0–0
D° of the Board of Admiralty..........	3–0–0
D° for Shipping Papers................	3–0–0
Devices & Checks for Certificates.......	2–0–0
D° for Bills of Exch°.................	3–0–0
D° for the New Currency in the Press....	5–0–0
The Great Seal of the States with a Reverse......................	10–0–0
	£45–0–0

£45 in hard money at
    60 for One is...................... £27–0–0²

Immediately after he had presented the bill, Hopkinson sent the Board of Treasury the following communication, which is referred to in the report as "letter N° 6":

Agreeable to the Expectations of the Board I this Morning exhibited an Account for certain Devices &c in which a Charge was...

The following is the final (dated June 24, 1780) invoice of three which he submitted dealing with 'labours of fancy', listing the items for which he requests payment, the amount in pounds.

From *Life and Works of Francis Hopkinson*, Hastings (1926), p. 243 from the *Papers of the Continental Congress*: He is denied compensation on the basis that he *"was not the only person consulted on these exhibitions of Fancy"* and that *"the public is entitled to those little assistances given by gentlemen who enjoy a considerable salary under*

Congress without fee or further reward." The 'considerable salary' would be after he was appointed Treasurer of Loans in 1778, at which time he resigned from the Naval Board and Marine Committee.

What is significant in this matter is that the critics did not disagree that he had submitted a design for a flag, clearly suggesting a number of people knew about it. The assumption has always been that it was offered three years before, at about the time the Flag Resolution was adopted, concurrently with his being on the Marine Committee and Naval Board in 1776-77. If this were the case, and the flag design had been accepted, it would be logical to assume that the purpose of the flag would have been well known and the name he attached to the design would not change from one invoice to the next. He would not call it "The Flag of the United States of America" in one case, and then "The Naval Flag of the United States." But if the design had not been accepted, or if it were supplied sometime after the date of the Flag Resolution with a different purpose in mind, it is reasonable that he is not consistent in naming the purpose for which the design is intended.

Furthermore, based on the monetary value he assigned to his design, it can be surmised that it was somewhat elaborate, with artistic elements that made it impractical. The circle of stars flag is too obvious to qualify as an artistic contribution by him. A more likely design would be a variation of his work on the Great Seal. Flags with the picture of an eagle with wings spread, painted on silk with a halo of stars above it begins to appear about the time of the great seal design. Could this be attributable to Hopkinson? He initially envisioned it as the Flag of the United States, but he may also have proposed it as a naval flag.

The authors of the *National Geographic* article (including Commander Bryon McCandless, U.S.N.), developed in some detail the travails Hopkinson was subjected to in seeking payment for his "Fancy" work including a flag design, but do not recognize Hopkinson as being responsible for the "new constellation" flag adopted in the Flag Resolution. They suggest that John Paul Jones, fresh from victories at sea and in Philadelphia at the time, influenced the legislators regarding the design for the flag, whatever the arrangement of stars that was intended. This assumption is based on the fact that the next resolution passed by the Board of War on that day put John Paul Jones in command of the *Ranger*, being built in Portsmouth, New Hampshire. However the flag Jones flies later in Europe has red, white and blue stripes. This is not what the Flag Resolution specifies, so it seems doubtful that Jones influenced the wording, and therefore should not be accorded any credit for the flag design.

Over time, dating from the October 1917 issue of the *National Geographic* and Hastings biography (1926), there has not been any consistent view of Hopkinson's role in the design of our first flags, as might be expected given the absence of evidence that his design was adopted.

Milo Quaife writes (1942), "*Hopkinson repeatedly asserted in writing, to men who had ample means of knowing the truth of the matter, that he had designed the flag; nor did his enemies on the Treasury Board deny it.*" Yet Quaife does not give him the credit for it. "*The question who conceived the idea of replacing the two crosses on the existing Great Union Flag with the thirteen stars 'representing a new constellation' still remains unanswered… Nor have we any information that any practical use was ever made of Hopkinson's drawing.*" Quaife evidently regards Hopkinson's suggested design as a contribution that was not utilized.

Notwithstanding, Quaife, et al (1961) go so far as to picture a *Conjectural Francis Hopkinson design for the Stars and Stripes* (Exhibit 27a) with *five-pointed stars* arranged in the 3-2-3-2-3 pattern. The authors make it clear that the flag conceived in the Flag Resolution was intended solely for marine use.

Struggling to give Hopkinson credit for something, Furlong and McCandless (1981) speculate that Hopkinson's design had six-pointed stars arranged in a pattern of 4-5-4 lines but they do not commit to this. Of course, this leaves open the question of who initiated the design with the stars in a circle.

Quaife (1942) is less than objective in dismissing the Betsy Ross story. Menezes (1997) describes how Quaife reviews Betsy's life story in a derogatory tone to diminish the significance of Canby's story, when in reality Quaife is attacking the symbolism of the Weisgerber painting and the feminist suggestions in its imagery.

In truth, there was no clear and definitive idea of what our national flag, or even our naval flag, looked like in the beginning. Twelve stars in a circle with one in the center, stars arranged 5-3-5, or irregularly arranged in three or four rows, were all acceptable. The version which ultimately caught on had the stars arranged 3-2-3-2-3, but while it would appear that the members of the Marine Committee and the

Board of War had an arrangement of the stars in mind when the Flag Resolution was passed, since no explanation had been offered, any flag maker could produce an arrangement of the stars and assert it was the "new constellation" intended by Congress.

Richardson (1982), while acknowledging Hopkinson's claim to be the designer of our national/naval flag, doesn't give him credit for the circle of stars. His position is that the arrangement of the stars in the canton was left for later congressional representatives to resolve.

Willis Fletcher Johnson (1930) is quite certain that regardless of whose design it is, Congress was acting on a design they were all aware of, in other words confirming what was already general knowledge. Johnson says, *"Perhaps the most noteworthy and the most significant circumstance connected with this great historical event was the apparent absence of comment upon it in Congress or elsewhere, either before or after its achievement… The substitution of the Stars and Stripes* (for the Grand Union Flag) *must be considered extraordinary, and explicable only on the ground that there was practically unanimous agreement upon the propriety and felicity of such action."* In this, Johnson is also making the point that adopting a unique flag, different from the Grand Union flag, was consistent with the action taken in declaring our independence from England.

Did Hopkinson, or did he not, create the "stars in a circle" design or did he have some other arrangement of the stars in mind? We have the thoughts of Hastings (1926, page 254) who writes, *"About the origin of the American flag we lack the definite and reliable information that we have about the origin of the Great Seal. Numerous writers have discussed the subject, but since most of them were more sentimental than scholarly, the chief results of their labors has been the wide dissemination of a romantic legend.* [The Betsy Ross Story?] *The name of the designer has never been discovered, and even the source of the design is a matter of dispute. Whoever may have been the designer of the national ensign, the evolution of the design itself can be pretty definitely traced."* And he goes on to cite the earlier flags from which the circle of stars flag would be a logical descendant.

However, in spite of this statement he is willing to give Hopkinson the credit for the design of the flag adopted June 14, 1777. Hastings (1939) asserts that it is incontrovertible that Hopkinson made the various designs for which he submitted his invoices. As to whether they were utilized is another matter. Hastings is unable to make a judgement regarding the design for the Great Seal since others worked on it and it was not adopted until several years after Hopkinson's invoice was submitted. But with respect to the flag design, he quotes Hopkinson's letter to the Board of Admiralty: *"I have with great readiness, upon several occasions exerted my small Abilities in this way for the public Service; and, as I flatter myself, to the Satisfaction of those I wished to please."*

Hastings concludes from the last phrase that Hopkinson's flag design was accepted. Hopkinson's position as Chairman of the Navy Board on the date the flag was adopted gives this weight. But can we conclude, as Hastings does, that credit for submitting a design leads to the conclusion that the design was accepted? This is not proven, and the only claim Hopkinson makes in his letter is that his seal for the Board of Admiralty was accepted. Wouldn't he have said more regarding his flag design?

The amount of money Hopkinson requested for his flag design as compared to his other work is indicative of what the imaginative and symbolically-oriented mind of Hopkinson would have designed as the *"Flag of the United States"*. His final invoice specifies an amount of **ten pounds for his work on the Great Seal** as Consultant to the Second Committee, and **nine pounds for his flag design.** Other items on the invoice are lesser amounts including only five pounds for one currency design "in print". If Hopkinson were to have proposed a simple flag design, such as the 3-2-3-2-3 star arrangement, or the 4-5-4, or even the circle of stars design, would this be something that he thought was worth nine-tenths as much as his detailed two-sided artistic work on the Great Seal? This author answers, *"No; he had something grander in mind."*

The United States Postal Service

On June 14, 2000 the United States Postal Service (USPS) issued, as part of its Classic Collection Series, a pane of stamps depicting 20 historic American flags described as *"linked to the evolution of the Stars and Stripes since 1775."* According to Linn's *U.S. Stamp Yearbook, 2000*, published by A. Baker and Taylor Company, the set was conceived by Richard Sheaff, one of the Postal Service's contract art directors and designers. *"Based upon his own research he chose 20 visually interesting and historically significant flags and made a sample of a Classic Collection pane to show to the Citizens' Stamp Advisory Committee."* They found it visually very exciting and suggested that PhotoAssist [the Postal Service's research firm] be engaged to find a vexillologist [flag expert] to review Sheaff's flags and make recommendations. The specialist selected was Dr. Whitney Smith of the Flag Research Center in Winchester, Massachusetts.

In the final finished pane of stamps were several recommended by Dr. Smith which replaced ones proposed by Sheaff. Included was a stamp labeled *Francis Hopkinson 1777*. The presumption was that this was the design proposed by Francis Hopkinson and adopted by the Continental Congress on June 14, 1777, the date that gave us today's Flag Day. The six-pointed stars were said to represent a "new constellation." Various reviews of the proposed stamp pane led to corrections in dates, and inquiries as to whether Francis Hopkinson's flag, with its circle of 13 white stars on the blue canton, was consistent with other authorities who said the 13 stars were actually arranged in alternating rows of 3-2-3-2-3. The Postal Service's Helen Skillman responded, telling Linn's that Hopkinson's *"exact design is not known and current thinking favors the ring of stars as the Hopkinson design, believed to have been in use from 1777 to 1795."* Skillman goes on to say; *"Although the 13 stars in circle is a popular design in the minds of most Americans, there is no proof that this was the design Francis Hopkinson proposed to Congress... The exact arrangement of the stars on the Hopkinson flag is not known."*

Unfortunately, the publication of this particular flag image (Exhibit 26b) in an otherwise accurate Classic Collection Series of stamp images lends credibility to an unproven "fact", i.e. a conjecture. Acknowledging some criticism of his recommendation of this stamp, Whitney Smith wrote, for the back of the stamp, the explanation that *"Continental Congress member Francis Hopkinson designed the first stars and stripes. His stars may have formed rows or a ring, the exact design is not known. In a resolution of June 14, 1777, they were said to represent a new constellation."*

The USPS allowed Dr. Whitney Smith to put forth a theoretical image which might be thought of as being a *conjectural flag design* in competition with earlier conjectural designs others had attributed to Francis Hopkinson. Of all the possible designs attributed to Hopkinson, this one is most consistent with his temperament and nature. However, the use of a circular arrangement for the stars was not necessarily new. The point is made by Rabbow (1980) that the Marine Committee could have had before them, when they acted, a relatively simple image (thus no need to describe it) consistent with at least four known flags: (1) the flag of the 2nd New Hampshire Regiment, (interlocked rings forming a circle), (2) the flag of the Independent Company of Newburyport (thirteen mailed hands holding an endless chain of thirteen links), (3) the flag of the First Troop Philadelphia Light Horse (central emblem with thirteen ribbons tied in a knot), and (4) the flag of the United Company of the Train of Artillery, a Rhode Island Regiment formed in 1775 (thirteen five-pointed stars in a circle surrounding an emblem including a snake and the words 'Do Not Tread on Me'.)

The "new constellation" flag, is unquestionably a design which became part of our national heritage, the symbolic flag of the new nation, despite the fact that it did not become widely utilized. In this respect, the conjectural *Hopkinson* stamp issued on June 14, 2000 was representative of the "Flag of the United States, 1777" depicted in the 1917 *Our Flag* issue of *National Geographic*. The flag design, however, is not confirmed to have been by Francis Hopkinson.

Chapter 13

The Great Seal and the "New Constellation"

*T*he meaning of the phrase "a new constellation" as used by the Marine Committee in the Flag Resolution may have been clear to them, but was left undescribed. It was interpreted for many years afterwards that any arrangement of stars in the canton could be said to represent a "new constellation." The significance of having the stars in a circle was not explained until William Barton, working for the Third Committee, produced his design for the Great Seal.

The development of a design for the Great Seal of the United States was a task undertaken by three successive committees of the Continental Congress. After the design proposed by the First Committee was rejected, a Second Committee was appointed and Francis Hopkinson was employed by this group as a consultant to prepare a design, which he did, but it was not accepted.

In his Great Seal design, Hopkinson employed a 'radiant constellation' of thirteen six-pointed stars above the spread wings of an eagle. His design (Exhibit 17a) is pictured in publication #10411, the Department of State, Bureau of Public Affairs, September 1996. This constellation of stars in his design carried over into the final image of the Great Seal, seen on the back of our dollar bill. In Hopkinson's drawing, the stars are inside a circle and while they might appear to be randomly placed, their layout evolved into a 1-4-3-4-1 arrangement. His design for the Great Seal could have been an adaptation of his proposed flag design. It is only a few years later the eagle with spread wings and a halo of stars above it begins to appear on flags.

The meaning of the term "new constellation" became clear when the Third Committee was appointed to design a Great Seal, and they engaged William Barton to produce a design. His first attempt was too complex to be useful and he was asked to do another drawing. According to Patterson and Dougall (1976), Barton's second Great Seal design includes an eagle holding a small stars and stripes flag, which is identified as "the ensign of the United States, proper," a flag with the stars in a circle. Barton writes, *"The stars, disposed in a circle, represent a new Constellation... Their disposition in the form of a circle denotes perpetuity, — eternity."* Although the Continental Congress also rejected Barton's second design it remains of interest because it is one of the earliest known illustrations of a United States flag with a circle of stars. It would appear to explain the term "a new constellation" which had been used by the Marine Committee in the Flag Resolution.

Barton's work for the Third Committee was submitted to Congress on May 9, 1782, and the matter was again referred to the Secretary, Charles Thomson. To quote Patterson and Dougall, *"In effect, Thomson was now a committee of one charged with preparing a design for the seal. With the reports, drawings, and other papers of the three committees in front of him, he set about producing a design of his own."* He selected the best features of the previous designs, left out details that cluttered the design, featured the eagle, and brought the design to the Continental Congress (Exhibit 17b). The cluster of six-pointed stars called by the Second Committee a "radiant constellation" remained, surrounded by clouds.

Richardson (1982) discusses the Seal as designed by Thomson, working from the earlier designs. He *"made a major contribution by greatly simplifying and thereby strengthening the design. Thus refined, it was submitted to the Continental Congress and adopted on June 20, 1782."* A die was made by Robert Scott of Philadelphia in 1782 and it remained in use for almost 60 years (Exhibit 17c).

An engraving of the Great Seal of the United States was made in 1786 by Robert Trenchard for publication in the *Columbian* magazine, presumably because the general public would not know what the seal looked like, as it was only being used on official documents. While there are minor differences between the engraving and the actual Great Seal, there is one major difference. The stars in the Trenchard engraving are five-pointed (Exhibit 17d), consistent with the argument that Betsy Ross had encouraged the adoption of five-pointed stars, as opposed to the heraldic six-pointed stars Hopkinson and others may have favored and which were often used.

The original die was in use until 1841, when it was replaced by one engraved in steel by John Peter Van Ness Throop of Washington, D.C. He engraved five-pointed stars instead of six-pointed ones, and this has been carried forward to this day. Quoting Richardson, *"The final version of the Seal appears on the present-day $1.00 bill; the central device is the American spread eagle (independence and strength) bearing a shield of thirteen red and white stripes (the states) supporting a blue horizontal bar (congress). The right talon clutches an olive branch; the other, thirteen arrows. Above the eagle is placed a constellation of thirteen five-pointed stars breaking through the clouds (a new nation)."*

Chapter 14

The Five-Pointed Star

Does Betsy Ross get credit for influencing the use of five-pointed stars in our national flag? Early flags had stars with four, six and eight points. Five-pointed stars begin to appear, as on the flag that flew over Fort Independence in Boston Harbor, towards the end of the war for independence. The stars on this flag are five-pointed, arranged in a 4-5-4 manner. It has never been subjected to textile and thread examination to verify its age although it is said to have been made in 1781 by Jonathan Fowle, a merchant of Boston, and presented to the fort, then Castle William, where his son was a member of the garrison. Prints of this flag show the canton in the upper right corner, rather than the left, because the reverse of the flag is being seen. The Massachusetts Art Commission advises that a backing was stitched to the flag to preserve it, with the result that it is a left-handed flag.

Another early flag with five-pointed stars would be the one carried by General John Stark at the Battle of Bennington, August 16, 1777. The canton of his flag is owned by the Bennington Historical Society and can be seen at its museum. According to *So Proudly We Hail*, the stars are in the 3-2-3-2-3 arrangement. In response to an inquiry, museum curator Stephen Perkins says the stars are of varying sizes and arranged in no particular pattern, so the imagery may be approximate.

Five-pointed stars appear in three items dating to 1783-1784. The first is a well-known engraving by the Connecticut inventor and engraver Abel Buel. He did a large wall map of the United States after the Treaty of Paris in 1783. This was advertised in the *Connecticut Journal* on March 31, 1784. The stars are five-pointed, arranged in the 3-2-3-2-3 fashion.

The second item is Major Pierre Charles L'Enfants' initial design for the diploma of the Society of the Cincinnati done in June 1783. To quote Furlong and McCandless, "It is an allegorical scene dominated by an armor-clad person holding a sword in his right hand and a flag in his left. The flag has thirteen stripes, the first and last of which are red. In the canton are thirteen five-pointed stars arranged in an oval."

The third item is also described by Furlong and McCandless, in a book published in Germany in 1783. Twelve copper plates depict incidents in the American Revolution. One of the twelve plates is of the flag of the United States showing stripes in a red, white, and blue sequence (the John Paul Jones influence) and five-pointed stars arranged in a 3-2-3-2-3 pattern.

From the same source, we learn that not all early publications support the five-pointed star, and this should be noted. A 1783 British book on naval flags includes an illustration of the United States flag with only red and white stripes, and with six-pointed stars in the 3-2-3-2-3 pattern. In London, the cartouche on a 1783 map of the United States by John Wallis shows the stars and stripes flag with thirteen four-pointed stars positioned horizontally in the 3-2-3-2-3 arrangement. While the number of points on the stars is not consistent with Betsy's suggestion, the arrangement of the stars is meaningful.

Clearly, the five-pointed star was initiated by somebody. It is reasonable that Betsy's flag could have been a major contributing factor in its adoption. Just as nobody denies Francis Hopkinson's claim to having submitted a design for a naval flag, no one has come forward to dispute Betsy's claim of having introduced the five-pointed star to the gentlemen who called on her that day. Although others could have independently come to favor five-pointed stars, no records have emerged to compete with Betsy's claim. Her 'committee' would have passed along her view that the five-pointed star should be used rather than the European heraldic six-pointed stars. If they mentioned Betsy as the source of this idea, it could help explain why the story of 'Betsy Ross' survived in folklore from the time of the Revolutionary War.

The Pattern for Stars Artifact

Betsy convinced her visitors that a five-pointed star would be easy to make. She demonstrated a very simple way to fold a piece of paper and with one cut produce a perfect five-pointed star. A sample folded five-pointed star pattern was shown by Reeves Wetherill of the Society of Free Quakers at a 1963 luncheon meeting of the Women's Committee of the Philadelphia Flag Day Association. Dr. Timmins (1981) subsequently published a picture of the original artifact. This *Pattern for Stars* (Exhibit 4) continues to be in the possession of the Society. Wetherill explained that the folded star pattern came from an old safe which his father had caused to be opened in 1922. Reeves Wetherill was a descendant of Samuel Wetherill, one of the founders of the Society of Free Quakers. The safe did not belong to Samuel, according to the present-day Clerk of the Society, but to a Wetherill of a later generation, but it is clear the artifact has been in the possession of someone associated with the Society of Free Quakers since the pattern was created. The Society of Free Quakers continues to exist as a philanthropic organization.

The folded paper is barely six inches long. It has been re-photographed by Robert Vaughan. A serious, albeit unsuccessful, effort, was made to find a handwriting match in the records and ledgers of the Society of Free Quakers (in the possession of the American Philosophical Society in Philadelphia) in an effort to determine just who might have created this intriguing item.

There are four lines of writing on the corner of the paper, in lead pencil, as follows:

> H. C. Wilson
> Betsey Ross
> pattern for
> stars —

Betsy is spelled as 'Betsey', and the 'H' appears to overwrite a 'W'. 'C. Wilson' would be Clarissa Wilson, who was widowed in 1812 and moved from Baltimore to live and work with Betsy. The reason for the 'H' requires some speculation. Could it represent Sophia Hildebrand, Clarissa's daughter?

There is little record of activities of the Society of Free Quakers after the early 1830s. Regular meetings for worship had ceased, yet in January 1847, there was a Meeting for Business at a private home on Market Street (Exhibit 19). The meeting appears to have been held to arrange for firewood and coal to be purchased and delivered to those who might be in need. Another item of business that would interest us is the recommendation that a fire-proof iron chest be purchased for the records of the Society.

Three names, Margaret Boggs, Clara Wilson, and Sophia Hildebrand, are grouped together and set apart from the others in the listing of people who attended this Meeting for Business. This suggests these three were not part of the social-economic groupings within the body of Friends at that time or they arrived late as a group. The three ladies mentioned (along with several others) each elected to receive several tons of coal.

[Boggs and Hildebrand would later testify to the 'Betsy Ross' story in support of William Canby.]

A separate Minute in the files (Exhibit 20) reports that on January 6, 1847, it was recorded by the Clerk of the Meeting, R. P. Wetherill, that the Free Quaker Dorcas Society was organized on December 19, 1845, and held weekly meetings at 419 Market Street until March. The Dorcas Society, named after a charitable woman in the Bible, was founded by Sarah Ward, wife of Rev. Daniel S. Ward, in 1824 in Newfoundland to make clothing for the poor. The concept spread to other religious bodies who organized their own groups to make clothing, under the name of the Dorcas Society. Apparently these Quaker ladies were so moved.

This is not the first time Quaker ladies had made garments for the poor. In earlier years, there are entries in the Minute Book of expenditures for fabric used to make garments which would have involved the volunteer seamstresses before they called themselves the Dorcas Society.

The Quaker ladies needed supplies for the Dorcas Society work, and the records show that "various items of cloth and tape, buttons, and needles" were purchased for said Society by the purchasing Committee for a total expenditure of $22.36. Seventy-two garments were made and distributed to the poor (Exhibit 20).

This activity would likely have involved only the youngest of the flag-makers. Margaret Boggs, Betsy's niece, would have been sixty-eight, and Clarissa Sidney Wilson, Betsy's daughter, would have been about 60 years old, so they may not have been active participants. Clarissa's daughter, Sophia Hildebrand, could have been active, although no records identify which ladies did the sewing. This charitable activity would have brought Sophia into a group of Quaker ladies who might have had only a limited knowledge of her background and occupation.

It is quite possible the conversation among the ladies turned to the role of Betsy Ross in making a flag for the 'committee,' a story which would be familiar to the other Quaker ladies. Sophia could have described to the group how her mother Clarissa, and her Grandmother Betsy Ross, had a simple way of making five-pointed stars (Exhibit 3). Perhaps she folded a piece of paper and made a partial cut.

We may speculate that when this Pattern for Stars was created, one of the ladies thought it should be preserved. Intending to note upon it the name of Clarissa Wilson, she makes a 'W' for Wilson. But before the name is written out, the writer decides that because it is Sophia Hildebrand who created the cleverly folded paper, her name should be on it and overwrites the 'W' with an 'H'. Sophia demurs to having her name on the Pattern for Stars, feeling that her mother's name should be on it and the writer allows the 'H' to stand, and follows it with 'C' for Clarissa and then spells out Wilson in full, followed on the next line by the name 'Betsey Ross'.

Speculation aside, this artifact is historically significant because the names of both Betsy Ross and her daughter Clarissa are linked to the folded Pattern for Stars. The inclusion of her daughter's name dates it to the period following 1812 (many years later than the making of the first flag) when Clarissa had joined Betsy in her upholstery shop making flags. We are left with several unknowns regarding this intriguing artifact: 1) the exact date it was made, 2) who preserved it through the years, and 3) the reason for the initial overwrite of the 'W' with an 'H'. The fact that Betsy is spelled as 'Betsey' suggests that the writer was not a family member (Exhibit 4).

Did the writer have prior knowledge of Betsy Ross' involvement in making the first flag, or was this communicated by Sophia? In any event, someone apparently recognized the demonstration piece was important enough to put in a safe for a later generation to discover.

Dr. Timmins (1983) believed the writing was by Clara Wilson herself, but the handwriting does not match with her signature on the receipt for the flag made for Mr. Rodney of Wilmington. This receipt is in the Rodney files in the Delaware Historical Society in Wilmington, and is dated in the spring of 1813, before the bombardment of Fort McHenry in Baltimore. Payment is signed for by Clarissa Sidney Wilson, Betsy's daughter, who had come into Betsy's household the year before. Mr. Rodney is Daniel Rodney, governor of Delaware from 1814-1817.

We can say with some certainty this sample pattern for five-pointed stars found its way into the iron fireproof chest authorized to be purchased at the January 1847 meeting, and that it has been in the possession of the Society of Free Quakers, or a Wetherill descendant, from the time it was made until the present, including its being brought out in 1963 by Reeves Wetherill. It is a significant artifact in support of the premise that 'Betsy Ross' initiated the use of the five-pointed star in our flags. Its significance is only increased by the absence of other physical evidence for competing claims.

Exhibit 1, page 43
Portrait of Betsy Ross (1752-1836) by Samuel L. Waldo, c. 1832

Exhibit 2, page 43 & 93
Back of canvas,
Portrait of Betsy Ross
(Signed) Samuel Waldo,
(Painted) 32 (1832)
Courtesy of the owner

Betsy's 5-step, 4-fold, 1-cut, 5-sided star

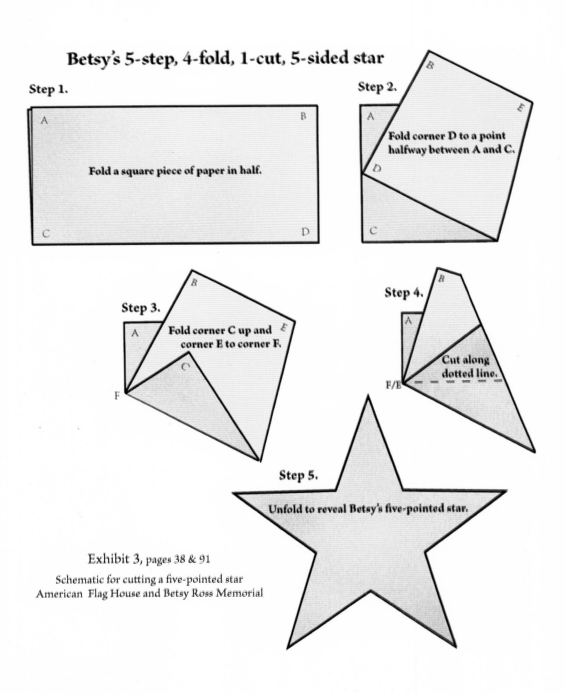

Step 1.

A   B

Fold a square piece of paper in half.

C   D

Step 2.

B

A   E

Fold corner D to a point halfway between A and C.

D

C

Step 3.

B

A   E

Fold corner C up and corner E to corner F.

C

F

Step 4.

B

A

Cut along dotted line.

F/E

Step 5.

Unfold to reveal Betsy's five-pointed star.

Exhibit 3, pages 38 & 91

Schematic for cutting a five-pointed star
American Flag House and Betsy Ross Memorial

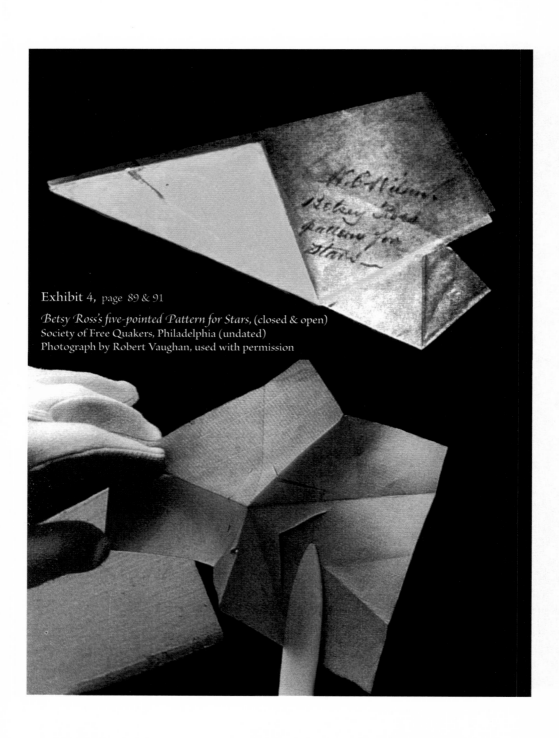

Exhibit 4, page 89 & 91

Betsy Ross's five-pointed Pattern for Stars, (closed & open)
Society of Free Quakers, Philadelphia (undated)
Photograph by Robert Vaughan, used with permission

Exhibit 5, page 19
Birth of Our Nation's Flag by Charles H. Weisgerber (1893)
Courtesy Charles H. Weisgerber II

Exhibit 6, page 42

Betsy Ross and the Flag Committee by Ellie (Sully) Wheeler, 1851
Courtesy of Weston Adams

Exhibit 7, pages 28 & 42

The Making of Our Flag by J. L. G Ferris (c.1900-1910)
Courtesy of the owner

Exhibit 8, pages 17 & 17 46

George Washington at Princeton, 1779
Charles Willson Peale (1741-1827) Oil on canvas.
The Pennsylvania Academy of the Fine Arts, Philadelphia, Pa.; used with permission.

Exhibit 9, pages 46, 47, 54, & 95

George Washington (1732-1799) at the Battle of Princeton, Jan. 3, 1777
Charles Willson Peale (1741-1827) oil; 237 x 144.5 cm (sight); 106 x 70in (frame)
Princeton University. Commissioned by the trustees. Photo credit Bruce M. White
Used with permission.

Five-pointed Stars

Was a 5-pointed circle-of-stars flag, as rendered by Peale, made by Betsy and flown at the Battles of Trenton and Princeton in January 1777?

Peale was there.

By 1783, Betsy's proposed 5-pointed stars appear on George Washington's uniform.

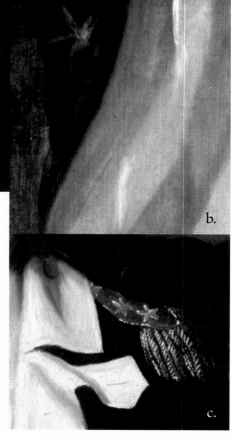

Exhibit 10

Details: *George Washington (1732-1799) at the Battle of Princeton, Jan. 3, 1777*
Charles Willson Peale
Princeton University. Commissioned by the trustees 1783-1784
Used with permission.
Photo credit Bruce M. White.
Pages 46 & 48

a. Detail of George Washington without the blue sash that signified his rank as commander in chief in former paintings.

b. Detail of Stars and Stripes flag with 5-pointed stars, presumably part of a circle.

c. Detail of three 5-pointed stars on epaulet that signify George Washington's rank.

Exhibit 11, pages 46 & 48

Detail: *George Washington (1732-1799) at the Battle of Princeton, Jan. 3, 1777*
Princeton University. Commissioned by the trustees 1783-1784. Photo credit Bruce M. White.

Please note that this image differs from others painted by Peale of this engagement.
In another, Washington is shown in the front rallying his men. This is reported in
in *Peale's Diary*, Appendix 5.

When Peale repeated versions of his first painting, *George Washington at Princeton*, 1779,
he updated Washington's uniform to reflect changes consistent with the General Orders
of the day as shown in Exhibits 8 & 9.

Resolved That the marine committee be impowered to
give such directions respecting the continental
ships of war in the river Delaware as they
think proper in case the enemy succeed in
their attempts on the said River.

Resolved That the Flag of the united states be 13 stripes alternate red and white, that the
Union be 13 stars white in a blue field represent-
ing a new constellation.

The Council of the state of Massachusetts bay
having represented by letter to the president
of Congress that capt John Roach sometime
since appointed to command the continental
ship of war the Ranger is a person of doubtful character and ought not to be intrusted
with such a command: therefore

Resolved That captain Roach be suspended
until the navy board for the eastern department shall have enquired fully into his character & report thereon to the marine committee.

Resolved That capt John Paul Jones be appointed
to command the said ship Ranger.

Resolved That William Whipple esqr member
of Congress and of the marine committee
John Langdon esqr continental agent and
the said capt John Paul Jones be authorised
to appoint the lieutenant and other commissioned & warrant officers necessary for
the said ship and that blank commissions

Exhibit 12, page 10

The Flag Resolution of June 14, 1777
Facsimile page from *Rough Journal of the Continental Congress*
Reprinted from *The Evolution of the American Flag* by George Canby and Lloyd Balderston (1909)

a.

Exhibit 13
Regimental Banners

a. *Bucks of America* flag, c.1787 by American
   School (18th century) Massachusetts
   Historical Society, Boston, MA, USA,
   Bridgeman Art Library. Page 18

b. *Second Rhode Island Regiment Banner*
   as depicted in *National Geographic*, October
   1917. Native Rhode Islanders served in the
   Battles of Brandywine, Trenton, and
   Yorktown. This flag may be seen in the
   Rhode Island Statehouse. Page 18

b.

RHODE ISLAND
396

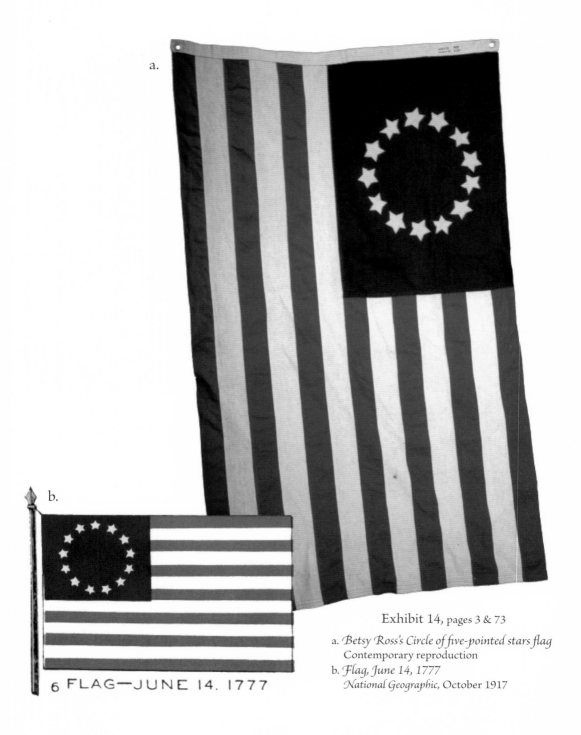

a.

b.

6 FLAG—JUNE 14. 1777

Exhibit 14, pages 3 & 73

a. *Betsy Ross's Circle of five-pointed stars flag*
   Contemporary reproduction
b. *Flag, June 14, 1777*
   National Geographic, October 1917

The resolution says nothing about the arrangement of the stars in the field. There is a tradition that in the first flag made the stars were placed as shown in the accompanying sketch, so that they outlined the two crosses which they replaced, as shown by the dotted lines in the

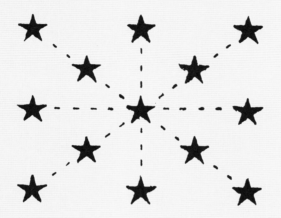

a.

sketch. But it is also known that on some of the earlier flags the stars were arranged in a circle, and this form is given by both Trumbull and Peale in their paintings of Revolutionary scenes.

Exhibit 15, pages 3 & 73

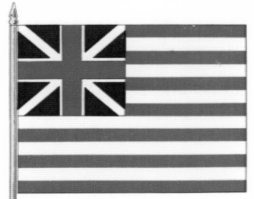

a. Pattern of five-pointed stars in canton reproduced from *The Evolution of the American Flag* by George Canby and Lloyd Balderston (1909).

b. *Grand Union or Continental Colors.* Sometimes considered the first flag of the United States, it was in use from late 1775 until mid 1777. Its blue canton was the red cross of the English St. George and the white Scottish St. Andrew. It is easy to see how the 3-2-3-2-3 pattern of stars was superimposed to replicate the pattern of the crosses. The 3-2-3-2-3 pattern is presumed to be easier to replicate on the hand sewn flags. Image from *National Geographic,* October 1917.

SCALE, 4V FEET TO AN INCH

Exhibit 16, page 45

Proposed Fresco, Ladies Waiting Room, (1856).
Courtesy Architect of the Capital, Washington, D.C.

a.

b.

d.

detail

c.

Exhibit 17 a, b, c, d, and detail, pages 83-84

a. Hopkinson's proposed design of the Great Seal, as consultant to the Second Committee.

b. Secretary of Congress, Charles Thomson's design of June 29, 1782

c. Great Seal of the United States as adopted by Congress in 1782. Impression from brass die possibly by Robert Scott of Philadelphia. It was in use for 60 years.

d. Robert Trenchard's engraving in 1786 representative of the Great Seal. Note that the stars are five-pointed. Courtesy American Philosophical Society, Philadelphia, Pa.

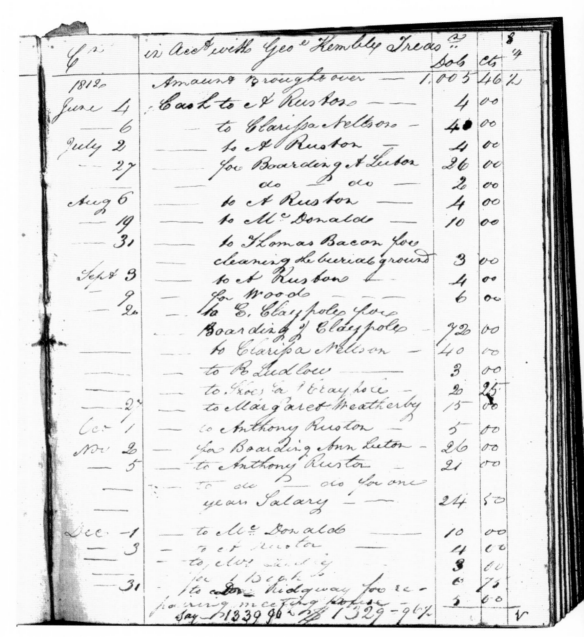

Cr	in Acct with Geoe Hembley Treasr	Dols	cts
1812	Amount Brought over —	1.005	46½
June 4	Cash to A Ruston — —	4	00
—— 6	—— to Clarissa Nellson —	40	00
July 2	—— to A Ruston —	4	00
—— 27	—— for Boarding A Luton	26	00
	—— do do	2	00
Aug 6	—— to A Ruston ——	4	00
—— 19	—— to McDonalds ——	10	00
—— 31	—— to Thomas Bacon for		
	cleaning the burial ground	3	00
Sept 3	—— to A Ruston —	4	00
—— 9	—— for Wood	6	00
—— 20	—— to E. Claypole for		
	Boarding J Claypole —	72	00
	—— to Clarissa Nellson —	40	00
	—— to R Ludlow	3	00
	—— to Shoes &a & Gray Lucie —	2	25
—— 27	—— to Margaret Weatherby	15	00
Octr 1	—— to Anthony Ruston	5	00
Novr 2	—— for Boarding Ann Luton —	26	00
—— 5	—— to Anthony Ruston —	21	00
	—— to do — do for one		
	year Salary — —	24	50
Dec —1	—— to McDonalds —	10	00
—— 3	—— to A Ruston ——	4	00
	—— to Mrs Ludley	3	00
—— 31	—— for 1 Bushls	6	75
	—— to Jno Ridgway for re-		
	pairing meeting house —	5	00
	Say $1339 96 — $ 1329 - 96½		

Exhibit 18, page 35

Ledger Page (1812), Society of Free Quakers, American Philosophical Society, Philadelphia

At a meeting of the Society of Free Quakers
held at the house of Mrs Gunnes Market Street
Jany. 20th 1847. The following members were present.

George D. Wetherill   John P. Wetherill Jr
Samuel W. Lippincott   Joshua Lippincott Jr
Timothy Bryan   Edward Wetherill
Saml Gunnes   Rachel Wetherill
Martha W Wetherill   Elizabeth Wetherill
Rebecca Gunnes   Mrs G. Wetherill
Sarah Ann Richard   Saly Wetherill
Moor de Mc Donald   Selmin Lippincott
A B. Wilson .   Charles Kimble

                    Margaret Boggs
                    Clara Welsh
                    Sophia Hildebran
The minutes of the last meeting were read & adopted.

Resolved that the committee &c. be authorized to
purchase an Iron fire proof chest for the papers of
the Society

Resolved that the clerk be and he is hereby authorized
to draw an order on the treasurer in favour of
Mrs Hampton for 20 dollars —

Com: on fuel delivered the following orders

Mrs Wilson   2 cords wood   Mr Richard   2   Selma Lippincott 4½ Tons Coal
Mrs Boggs   2   Charlotte Lippincott 2   J. P. Wetherill   4½
Mrs Kimble   2   Mrs Gunnes   2   J. W. Hildebran   4½
Mr Wilson   2   Mr J S Wetherill 2   Dorcas G Dow   Charlotte   4½
                              Mary Lips —   4 mel   Wilson 8 Tons   4½ Boggs   3½
                                                     Kimble 2½   Richard 2½
                                                         20 Tons

On motion of Saml Lippincott it was proposed to enquire into the
muscles of Mrs Murry. James Mallbert & Mrs Carey late B. Tripp
On motion resolved that the com. are hereby authorized to call a meeting
of the Society soon as they are prepared to report   Joshua Lippincott Jr
            adjourn   Clerk P.T.—

January 6th 1847.

The Free Quaker Dorcas Society was organized on the 19th of December 1845 at No 519 Market Street and held weekly meetings until March. during that time the following articles were purchased for said Society, by the purchasing Committee

	$	cts
46½ yds of Red Flannel at 23½ cts per yd	10	92
40 ¾ yds of Muslin at 8½ cts per yd	3	46
30 ½ yds of Canton Flannel at 11½ cts per yd	3	50
Bind Cotton Tape, Buttons & Needles	1	20
Chintz Muslin &c	3	28
	$ 22	36

72 Garments were made and distributed by this Society to the Poor. — Signed by the Treasurer
R P Wetherill

Received March 1845 of Rebecca Gumbes. Nineteen Dollars and eight cents for articles purchased for the Society — $ 19.08 cts R P Wetherill

Exhibit 20, page 90

Minute of meeting of the Free Quaker Dorcas Society, January 6th, 1847
Recording purchase of materials, American Philosophical Society, Philadelphia

The First United States Flag

Combining the 13 stars and 13 stripes, was made by Mrs. JOHN ROSS

In this house, 239 Arch Street, - Philadelphia, Pa., 1776.

(House still stands.)

We Certify This picture, copyrighted by C. W. Smith, of Philadelphia, correctly represents the house No. 239 Arch Street, Philadelphia, as it now appears, in which the first United States Flag of thirteen stars and thirteen stripes was made by our grandmother MRS. JOHN ROSS, under the direction of a Committee of the Continental Congress of which her husband's uncle, Colonel George Ross, one of the signers of the Declaration of Independence, was Chairman. It was made from a design furnished by General Washington in person, which she modified by changing the form and arrangement of the stars, and the given proportion of the Flag.

COPYRIGHTED C. W. SMITH.

George Canby   Mary Canby Culin.
Mary Sidney Garrett

Exhibit 22, page 24

Photograph: Betsy Ross House, c. 1920s, photographer unknown.
Note that in the early images, the building sits in a row of shops and that the double doors are on the left.
The building(s) to the left were purchased c. 1929 and razed to create a courtyard. Following
the renovation in late 1937-1941, the house now appears as it does in Exhibit 23.

Exhibit 23, page 24

Betsy Ross House, 239 Arch Street, Philadelphia, Pa. c. 2005
Digital rendering, photographer unknown.
House is said to have been restored to c. 1777.

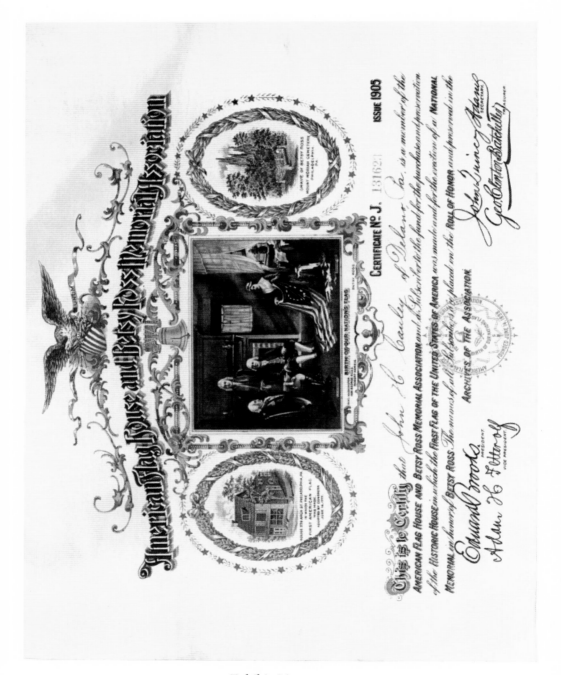

Exhibit 24, page 22
Certificate of Membership
American Flag House and Betsy Ross Memorial Association, issued 1905

THE BETSY ROSS HOU

a.

b.

FIRST DAY OF ISSUE

PHILADELPHIA
JAN 2
9-AM
1952
PA.

W.H.Schelmeyer
Apt. 2 - 1521 - Grape
Denver, Colorado.

FIRST DAY OF ISSUE

200th Anniversary
of the Birth
of BETSY ROSS

BETSY ROSS MAKING THE
FIRST AMERICAN FLAG

Exhibit 25, page 19

a. Graphic, c. 2000

b. *Envelope, First Day
of Issue of Besty Ross
Commemorative Stamp,*
Jan. 2, 1952
(Actual size)

a.

Francis Hopkinson Flag 1777
Continental Congress member
Francis Hopkinson designed the
first Stars and Stripes. His stars
may have formed rows or a ring;
the exact design is not known.
In a resolution of June 14, 1777,
they were said to represent
"a new constellation."

Francis Hopkinson Flag USA33
1777

b.

Exhibit 26

a. *Betsy Ross, Birth of Our Nation's Flag,* Commemorative Stamp, January 2, 1952 Displayed with permission. All Rights Reserved. Written authorization from the Postal Service is required to use, reproduce, post, transmit, distribute or publicly display these images. Page 19

b. *Francis Hopkinson's Flag 1777 Commemorative Stamp,* June 14, 2000 (Design is Conjectural) Stamp Designs ©2003 United States Postal Service. Displayed with permission. All Rights Reserved. Written authorization from the Postal Service is required to use, reproduce, post, transmit, distribute or publicly display these images. Page 80

Conjectural Francis Hopkinson design for the Stars and Stripes

a.

b.

Exhibit 27

a. *Conjectural Francis Hopkinson design for the Stars and Stripes,* Quaife, Weig and Appleman, (1961)
©1961 The Eastern National Park and Monument Association by Permission of HarperCollins Publishers, Inc.
Page 77

b. *Spirit of '76* Commemorative Stamp, Stamp Designs ©2003 United States Postal Service. Displayed with
permission. All Rights Reserved. Written authorization from the Postal Service is required to use, reproduce, post,
transmit, distribute or publicly display these images. Page 26

Exhibit 28, page 44

Elizabeth Claypoole, a.k.a. Betsy Ross
Portrait from the John Frederick Lewis Collection (circa 1830).

Print and Picture Collection, The Free Library of Philadelphia

a.

b.

Exhibit 29, *Family Portraits*, pages 28 & 43

a. *Jane Claypoole Canby*, 1792-1873 (daughter of Betsy).

b. *Elizabeth Canby*, born 10-10-1820, unmarried, died 1898,
Second child of Jane Claypoole and Caleb Canby.
Granddaughter of Betsy, and said to look like her.

Exhibit 30, page 34

Clarissa Sidneyy Claypoole Wilson (b 4/3/1785—d 7/10/1864)

by Manuel Joachim de Franca, 1830
Courtesy American Flag House and Betsy Ross Memorial

Exhibit 31, page 67

Sherman Quilt 1907
Made by the Ladies
of the
Rebecca Prescott Sherman Chapter
Minneapolis D.A.R.
organized 1907

*Green Silk in center
is from dress of Rebecca Sherman.*

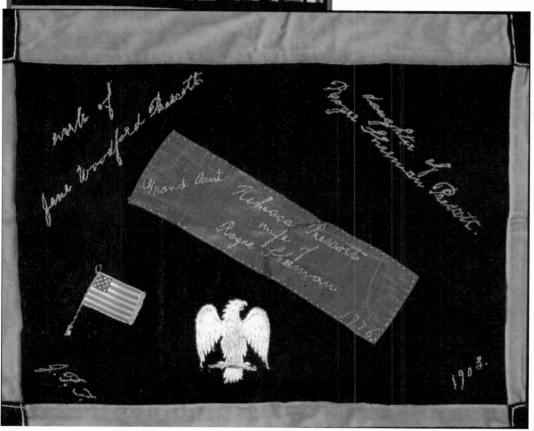

Exhibit 32, page 28

Gertrude Wilson, great great granddaughter of Betsy

Written on the back of photograph:

Gertrude Wilson (as Betsy Ross) August 8, 1895. Miss Gertrude Wilson, great-great granddaughter of Betsy Ross, wearing the clothes like those her great-great grandmother wore when she made the first flag.

Chapter 15

To Sum It Up

W e must recognize that the significance of our national flag evolved over time. In hindsight, more significance has been attached to the Flag Resolution than would have been warranted at the time. As the nation looked back upon the period of the Revolutionary War, it was assumed that there had always been a national flag. Certainly, the bombardment of Fort McHenry, and the poem, *The Star Spangled Banner,* which followed, cemented the significance of a national flag in the minds of the citizens of the United States. Moving forward to the period of the 1890s and the patriotic fervor that existed then, it is no surprise that the Betsy Ross story assumed a mythological status, and was accordingly prone to inaccuracies of fact.

For more than 100 years after Canby's speech, only the family story was available to document the role Betsy played in making the first flag. Since 1975, numerous discrete pieces of evidence that pre-date Canby's 1870 speech have emerged to substantiate the family story and validate its accuracy. This chapter provides a brief recapitulation of the key items which are seen to vindicate the family story of Betsy Ross's role in the creation of the 'first flag' and to establish that the 1992 *Wall Street Journal* article cited in the Foreword is not defensible as a well-researched piece.

The first item is the painting by Samuel Waldo in 1832 of the elderly woman he identified as 'Betsy Ross' (Exhibit 1). The identification is on the back of the canvas (Exhibit 2). The painting is not one of his more impressive portraits, it is smaller in scale and not as detailed, but he signed and dated it. Clearly, some folklore drew him to locate Betsy, likely at the home of a daughter, and take the time to paint her, but then keep the painting in his portfolio (her heirs knew nothing about it).

The second item is a painting of an elderly Betsy with flags in the background, by an unknown artist who made an effort to make her look younger. This painting was known to Betsy's descendants who argued that it couldn't really be her, as the likeness is poor. These doubts notwithstanding, the painting apparently is of Betsy, and it was used commercially after William Canby's speech.

The Ellie Wheeler painting of 1851 (years before Canby's speech) depicts the scene described by Betsy of the visit of the three men. Based on folklore, it predates the story affirmed by the testimonies. It also connects the circle of stars flag to Betsy.

The Pattern for Stars artifact was produced in a time and place that cannot be established, but certainly predates the Canby speech. It confirms Betsy contributed the idea of a five-pointed star for our naval and national flags. By the year 1794, this understanding was the norm.

Another piece of artistic evidence of the existence of folklore based on the Betsy Ross experience, which only recently came to light, is the incomplete design for the Ladies Waiting Room in the Capitol Building in Washington, D.C. It predates the speech by William Canby and it can only be judged on its own merits (Exhibit 16).

Two challenging items have recently come to light: The oral history of Rebecca Prescott Sherman and her interaction with Betsy Ross in making a flag for Washington, and the documentation that Captain Edward Williams carried a Betsy Ross flag (his description) to Mexico and flew it over the Fortress of Chapultepec in 1847. These items are new evidence that Betsy Ross was recognized as having a role in the making of our first flags. Both predate the speech by William Canby, and provide independent support of the family legend.

It was the 1893 painting by Charles Weisgerber *Birth of Our Nation's Flag* that indelibly linked the circle of stars flag to Betsy. At that time, there was no other claimant to that design, and it was our *symbolic* flag. If the house in which Betsy made that flag was to be saved, the time was ripe for John Quincy Adams, descendant of two Presidents, and Charles Weisgerber to go into business together and enlist a group of prominent Philadelphians to raise the money to buy the house in which they believed Betsy had met with the three men and in which the first flag had been sewn.

I believe that the first flag had the stars in a circle, laid out by Washington in Betsy's parlor using Betsy's suggestion of five-pointed stars. His headquarters banner initially had a circle of six-pointed elongated stars. Later, the same type of star is arranged in the 3-2-3-2-3 design in his headquarters banner.

The circle of stars flag was certainly known to the men in Philadelphia by the fall of 1776, if not sooner. The discussion at that time had to do with whether or not the Commodore of the Continental Navy would be in command of the Pennsylvania Navy as well. This did not happen, which created the situation that resulted in Betsy making colours for the Pennsylvania Navy. The flag she made to Washington's design was the one adopted by the Marine Committee of the Continental Congress as their naval flag.

Peale's painting of Washington at the Battle of Princeton (Exhibit 9) includes the flag Betsy made for Washington, confirming its existence. It was not a flag for the army or the navy, but intended to represent the developing nation, superseding the Grand Union flag. Betsy's involvement with the origin of this flag gave her flag-making career its start, and in time the legend evolved, something I'm sure she was not concerned about.

In Weisgerber's construction of his famous painting, it is the *symbolic flag* that resulted in citizens venerating Betsy, and which gave newly arrived immigrants the feeling that they were "Americans" as they recited the Pledge of Allegiance to the Flag of the United States. This feeling endures to the present as immigrants become citizens and see themselves as "Americans" regardless of their origin or ancestry.

Developments After 1783

Congress, on January 13, 1794, added two stars and two stripes to the flag. In the discussion of this change, a Mr. Watts suggested that a clause be added to the motion altering the flag to *establish* the new flag as "Flag of the United States", and would have precluded future alterations. The initially proposed changes to the flag, without his suggested clause, were enacted and it is this design, with five-pointed stars, which flew over Fort McHenry. This was the first time that the national flag was approved by the Congress of the United States.

It is quite reasonable to speculate that until 1794, there was no serious consideration being given to a national flag. Following the European tradition, flags were for marine or military use. In private correspondence, Mark Summers, historian for Jamestown-Yorktown Foundation, makes the point that the introduction of thirteen stars into the canton in place of the British jack did not symbolize that we were one nation. Up until the constitution was adopted in 1787, there were thirteen separate states, each retaining its own identity, united in the struggle against Britain while operating under the Articles of Confederation. It was only when the Articles of Confederation proved to be politically impossible that the leadership came together to forge a fresh constitutional document.

The flag for the Army that Washington regularly asked about in correspondence with the War Board didn't become available until the war was over, and was not distributed. Its design is not known. The first time an army unit flew a national flag was when a small unit, known as the Legion, was reconstituted on October 3, 1787. This new army unit had a blue flag, with an eagle and eight-pointed stars filling the center of the flag, and no stripes. This flag is illustrated in Quaife (1961), who attributes the research in this matter to Thruston (1926).

After the Revolutionary War, ships sailed displaying state flags. It was only when the Treaty of Algiers was signed in 1795 with the Barbary Pirates, who would only recognize one national flag and not state flags, that American ships sailing in foreign waters were required, under an act of Congress on June 1, 1796, to carry a passport that depicted the American Standard, and that they would fly that standard for recognition purposes (Moeller 1992). While no pictorial record exists of that standard, this was only a few years after the adoption by Congress of the flag with fifteen stars and fifteen stripes. According to Moeller (2002), evidence from engravings and paintings reveals that there were multiple versions of the American flag in use on land and sea after the adoption of the Flag Resolution on June 14, 1777, and even after our sovereignty was confirmed in 1783.

The 3-2-3-2-3 arrangement of five-pointed stars is illustrated in the 1793 painting of the flag flown by the Philadelphia-built ship, the *Pigou*, stopped by a French privateer (J. Welles Henderson Collection).

In the war of 1812, the army carried a flag with seventeen red and white stripes on the eagle's breast and seventeen stars above and around the eagle. The stars were five-pointed. This Army flag was not changed until 1834.

The flag had to be revised again in 1818 to recognize the new states that had joined the Union. To design a new flag, Congress called on Captain Samuel Chester Reid, a naval hero of the war of 1812. Captain Reid had been in command of a privateer called the *General Armstrong* and had gone into Fayal, Portuguese Azores (a neutral port) for fresh water. While he was there, three British ships under the command of Commodore Robert Lloyd sailed into port and demanded Reid's surrender. With the odds against him, Reid and his men defended themselves and their ship, and held off the British. Reid and his men then took up defensive position on shore, which caused the British to abandon their efforts to capture him. Instead, a group of British Officers met with Reid at the British Consulate to honor him with cheers and toasts (Loeffelbein, 1996).

Loeffelbein says, *"Congress asked Reid to produce a workable, lasting design for the national banner. He and his wife made up a model, returning to the original 13 stripes for the original 13 states, with a blue field to which a new star could be added for each new state."*

The bill President Monroe signed into law provided that stars representing new states would be added on July Fourth of the year following their admission into the Union. At that time, twenty stars were arranged in four rows of five to represent the twenty states. A basic pattern was set for our national flag, but it was not binding on flag makers. Both before and after this date, there were many variations in the layout of the stars. In some instances, they were arranged in lines or circles, or the stars were made into a single large star.

A 1968 publication of marine paintings from the collection at the Peabody-Essex Museum (Salem, Massachusetts) includes three paintings (1799-1800) by the artist William Ward. One flag has fifteen stars in three lines of five. Another has the fifteen stars arranged in a circle of fourteen with one in the center, and the last painting has stars arranged in lines of 4-4-4-3. All three flags depict five-pointed stars.

This collection has two paintings of the *U. S. Constitution*. The first painting (1815) depicts two flags, one having fifteen stars in three lines of five, the other having fourteen stars in a circle and a single star in the center. The other painting is of the battle between the *U.S. Constitution* and *H.M.S. Java* (painting date not given) and depicts two flags, both with three lines of five stars. All stars in both paintings are five-pointed.

In this same collection, paintings include the flags on sailing vessels of different types in the time period between the War of 1812 and 1840. A typical flag design is the stars in a circle with a five-pointed star in the center although in one case the stars are arranged to form a star. The artists may or may not have been present when each pictured event took place, but they certainly knew what flags of the period looked like.

In Conclusion

Whatever the origin of the arrangement of the stars, we have clear evidence both that the five-pointed star became firmly established, and that written and artistic records support the Betsy Ross family story giving her credit for recommending the five-pointed star.

Some present-day revisionists would ignore or deny the validity of the Betsy Ross family story, suggesting that either Benjamin Franklin or Francis Hopkinson, and not George Washington, was in the threesome that visited Betsy, and some would alter the date of the visit to a later time to fit another theory. None of these ideas work.

Historians who have a problem with the story do not have a defensible alternative in the record to explain Betsy being *selected by and paid by* the Pennsylvania State Navy Board for making 'colours' for the fleet. Furthermore, any assertion that the story is essentially mythological is demeaning to the character of Betsy herself, and to those descendants who have testified to the story. Throughout their history, Quakers have affirmed, rather than sworn to, statements of fact, because they are bound by faith to be truthful at all times. The custom of swearing oaths implicitly presumes that only sworn testimony needs to be truthful.

Francis Hopkinson is brought into the picture by people who choose to reject the Betsy Ross story. Those who were in a position to know did not deny Hopkinson's claim to having provided a design for a flag. However, no folklore exists to support a claim that Hopkinson's design was accepted.

There is a common link to five separate people identifying Betsy Ross as involved with the making of the first flag. That link is the time, fifty years later, when our country was remembering the Revolution. Three individuals, Ellie Wheeler, Edward Williams, and Emaunuel Leutze grew up in Philadelphia during the time Betsy was involved in flag making and apparently were aware of folklore about Betsy that existed even then. Later, Wheeler painted the scene (Exhibit 6) of the presentation of the first flag to the 'committee'; Williams asserted that he "borrowed" a Betsy Ross flag to take to Mexico; and Leutze used the circle of stars flag in his "Washington Crossing the Delaware" painting. In the same time period, the artist Samuel Waldo (Exhibit 1) and the unknown artist (Exhibit 28) painted Betsy Ross. In addition to this, we have the "Pattern for Stars" artifact in the possession of the Society of Free Quakers, which may well have dated to that period. This is not coincidence.

Several truths emerge. Two early flags and their multiple variations came into being. Both played a role in helping people see themselves as 'Americans.' Elizabeth Claypoole, a.k.a. Betsy Ross, was part of that process from the beginning, and her spunk and independent spirit has captured the imagination of generations. 'Betsy Ross' became a legend in her own time and remains so in our time.

Appendixes

Appendix I

Life of John Claypoole

Abstract from the publication, *Genealogy of the Claypoole Family in Philadelphia* (1893) by Rebecca Irwin Graff, published by J. B. Lippincott Co., being George Canby's recollections of the life of his grandfather John Claypoole as communicated by his mother, Jane Claypoole Canby and other family members.

There appear to be no records of his early life, but the recollections of him after he arrived at maturity represent to have been possessed of a marked degree of intelligence, a good memory, with pleasing and interesting powers of conversation, exhibiting in a fair measure the moderate educational advantages of his time. He was a keen observer of events, and had considerable ability as a writer, although, unfortunately, but few of his letters, and only fragmentary scraps of his literary efforts, have been preserved. His ready expression was sometimes shown in rhyming phrase, and some of his compositions in song and poem were of no mean order.

Notwithstanding John Claypoole's descent from well known Quaker ancestry, his parents were not, nor was he, a member of the Society of Friends. He was still quite a young man at the commencement of the Revolutionary War, and whatever troublesome particles of hereditary peace principles may have been floating in his Quaker blood, they proved but as straws in the current, and, for a time at least, were lost in the patriotic outburst which carried our forefathers on to American Independence. This impulse led him into the service of his country, and we find on record (in Pennsylvania in the Revolution, 1775-1783, Vol. I) that he received his commission as Second Lieutenant September 18, 1777.

He was wounded at the battle of Germantown by the flying fragments of a gun-carriage, which at the time he made light of, but the results of which may have increased the infirmity from which he suffered in later years.

At Red Bank he was the bearer of important dispatches to Washington. Here he came in contact, as he rode over the field, with numbers of wounded and dying Hessians, whose appeals for care and safety awakened his pity and commiseration. Upon questioning some of these miserable hirelings in their sad plight, as best he could, as to why they had left their homes to assist in the war and try to kill the Americans, who were their friends, he received an answer he was fond of frequently repeating: 'Hesse no kill; Hesse shoot low.'

After completing a term in the army, he took a position on board the 'Luzern,' an armed cruiser of eighteen guns, and sailed under letters of marque November 7th, 1780, for Port L'Orient, France. The 'Luzern' on her return voyage was captured by an English privateer, the 'Enterprise' mounting thirty-two guns, on April 4th, 1781. He, with other prisoners who refused to enter the English service, was landed at Limerick, on the river Shannon, in Ireland, and sent under guard across country to Cork, placed on board a guard-ship, and then conveyed to Plymouth, England, where he was committed to Old Mill Prison, July 6th, 1781, charged before a Justice of the Peace with High Treason, being found in arms, and in open rebellion against his King upon the High Seas.

Amongst the recollections of interest which were narrated by him, were incidents concerning his military and other experiences, his capture and travels above alluded to, the varied scenes and events of his prison life, with the sufferings endured in the presence of an alarming sickness which broke out and extended with fearful rapidity. One incident, which has been recorded by others and is worth repeating here, was the manner in which the joyful news of the surrender of Lord Cornwallis was conveyed into the prison by a newspaper concealed inside a loaf of bread which a sympathizing baker had furnished with his usual supply. The tumultuous demonstrations of delight, awakened in the hitherto saddened hearts of the prisoners, completely mystified their keepers, who, ignorant of the cause of the sudden outburst of wild glee and mad behavior, evinced by tearing off and whirling their coats, throwing their hats up in the air and making a deafening *din by their shouting, had good reason for supposing that the Yankees had all become suddenly insane.*

Shortly after John Claypoole's commitment to Mill Prison, his friend Captain Joseph Ashburn, who had left his young wife in Philadelphia, was also brought there a prisoner. George Canby digresses at this point to tell the story of Betsy, her marriage to John Ross, his death, Betsy being called upon by the 'committee' and how the flag was made with five-pointed stars; how Colonel Ross brings her word that the flag was accepted and gives her a large (for those days) note with which to purchase material and proceed making flags.

George Canby also comments with regard to the recall of the events of that moment "When we remember the disordered condition of public affairs at that time, and the great diversity of feeling which existed in the minds of even serious-minded folks in regard to the important events transpiring, it is not to be wondered at, that little note was made of interesting events, the actors in which did not realize their historical importance. It is, however, an important fact to chronicle that the business of flag-making, as established at that time by Betsy Ross, was continued by her and her immediate family for some sixty-odd years."

Captain Ashburn fell a victim, in Mill Prison, to the prevailing contagion, and after a short illness died, March 3d, 1782. In his unfortunate captivity, in company with and cared for in his sickness by his old friend John Claypoole, he naturally had much to say of his far-away busy and faithful wife, and in his dying moments confided to him his final farewell messages to her. These, on his release and return to Philadelphia, John Claypoole hastened to deliver in person, and was obliged to break to her the first sad tidings of her husband's death.

It is said that before Betsy Ross became the wife of Captain Ashburn, John Claypoole had already formed a strong attachment for her, so that it is not difficult to understand, aided by the tender sympathies elicited through the above-mentioned circumstances, that the gentle graces of the still young woman should have completely captivated his heart. He therefore earnestly pressed his suit and received her early consent to the union.

They were married May 8th, 1788.

Elizabeth Claypoole continued her upholstering and flag-making business. Her husband received an appointment for a time in the U.S.Custom House, and was known as a Custom House Officer; exactly in what capacity is not at present understood. They continued to live at the little Arch Street house for some three years after their marriage, when they removed to Second Street above Dock, and afterwards to Front Street, where their growing family of daughters was reared.

John Claypoole's health, never robust after the experiences heretofore related of his early years, completely broke down at, perhaps, the age of forty-five, when, after a stroke of paralysis, he was left a confirmed invalid and a cripple to the end of his life. This was the only condition in which his youngest daughter, the writer's mother, born in 1792, remembered him. She was fond of affectionately recalling incidents of his genial disposition, and had many pleasant little anecdotes to tell in relation to her father, and how he ever endeavored to brighten the affliction under which he suffered.

She especially took pleasure in repeating, amongst other things, some homely lines of a verse, which she used to say her father composed in his sleep, or, to speak more reverently, were given to him in a dream to help reconcile him to his invalid condition. Although suffering and unable to work, or to attend to business, he was able to walk about, and was in the habit of strolling abroad for exercise, and to while away the time. One night he dreamed that he was walking through a country neighborhood and drawing near to a place of worship, from which came the sound of voices singing, and as he paused somewhere close by and listened, there came to his ear these words:

"Why should we mortals vex ourselves with trouble, care and woe,

  When so much pleasure we can find walking to and fro?"

His daughter used to say that he found these lines a solace ever afterwards in moments of unrest and annoyance on account of his helplessness.

John Claypoole's bold signature and the small delicate one of his wife, Elizabeth Claypoole, are inscribed in the Record Book to the 'Declaration of Principles' of the Society of Free Quakers, of which they became members.

The remains of John Claypoole and his wife Elizabeth were buried in the Free Quaker Burying Ground, on the west side of Fifth Street, south of what is now Locust Street where they remained until the autumn of 1857, when they were removed to a lot in Mount Moriah Cemetery, purchased by their eldest daughter, Mrs. Clarissa Sidney Wilson, who, left a widow in 1812, had succeeded to the flag-making business of her mother, which had never been interrupted, and which she did not entirely abandon until a short time before her removal to Fort Madison, Iowa (1857), where she died, July 10th, 1864. (George Canby)

Appendix 2

Success Farm

A previously unpublished story about Betsy is in a paper describing "Success Farm" in Maryland. It is supplied by The Historical Society of Cecil County, Elkton, Maryland. It is based on an interview with Miss Belle Nickle who was descended from the Cromwell family who owned the farm in earlier years. The interview was probably prior to 1950. It is an interesting bit of hearsay about Elizabeth (Betsy) Claypoole whose third husband was related to the important Cromwell family. Herewith some relevant material from the history of "Success Farm."

High atop a hill overlooking the Conowingo Dam (Maryland) is the site of the once stately mansion of Success Farm. It is located about ten miles north of Port Deposit, off of Rt. 222. The house on the farm was said to have been built about 1734. The land was part of a huge grant (32,000 acres) to George Talbot by Charles Calvert, second son of Lord Baltimore. In the succession of owners of the property is John Hammond Cromwell, descended from Thomas Cromwell of England. The Cromwells owned "Success" for only one generation, as Cromwell had only girls and no sons to carry on the Cromwell name and the management of "Success"

John Cromwell was a man of remarkable energy and activity, a man of wealth and prominent in the affairs of the church. The farm was 400 acres of fertile farmland, a store and mill, and barns, stables, an ice house, wagon shed, corncrib and poultry house. [The house is described in detail, including a description of a huge 5' by 12' fireplace.] *In the early days, to heat the house horses had to draw the logs up to the back door from where they were rolled onto the huge slabs of the hearth. The house had a five cornered room, built in that shape, because of the huge fireplace. This room was always known as the "Betsy Ross" room.*

Apparently the story about Betsy was folklore known to two sisters, Belle and Mary Nickle. The name Nickle comes into the story because a daughter of J. H. Cromwell, Matilda, married Lewis Harlen, and they had a daughter, Mary Hammond Harlen, who married Andrew Nickle. Belle and Mary were the youngest and third youngest of the Nickles' twelve children. These sisters lived at "Success" for many years. In 1937 Mary died there at the ripe old age of 89. Belle survived her.

The Story:

> John Claypoole, one of Betsy's suitors, visited this house frequently. He was a cousin of John Hammond Cromwell, the owner. It was John, who, in describing the room, gave Betsy the idea which eventually led to the adoption of a five-pointed star, instead of the six-pointed star suggested by George Washington. In this room Cromwell entertained his visitors and young Claypoole had to sit and listen while his father and the owner of the house talked of the affairs at the farm and the latest news from the "City of Brotherly Love" where the Claypooles lived.
>
> It was hard for John Claypoole to hold Betsy's attentions with her other suitors. So John often made up games to entertain her. The room's design, as John reproduced it, looked like a star with five points; stars then usually had six points. Betsy made up a trick of cutting the five-pointed star out of paper with one deft cut. It was just a game and Betsy soon forgot it, until George Washington came for a flag.
>
> Many times after Betsy married Claypoole, Betsy visited the Cromwells at "Success." She enjoyed these glimpses of plantation life, [the writer then goes on to describe the plantation, and finally his/her search for the physical remains of the farm. The foundation is located, (the buildings had been torn down in the 1950s), and a few yards to the northeast of the foundation stands the tombstone bearing Cromwell and Dorsey inscriptions, nestled among the few of the once many boxwoods. The writer continues.] This is certainly a sad fate for the estate once so alive with activity.

[The story told here comes from the Nickle sisters, who heard it in the family, so it is hearsay, but interesting in the light of what others have said of Betsy, that she never traveled outside of Philadelphia. She could have been motivated to travel to the farm with her husband and children to avoid the heat of the city. The location described here is many miles south of Philadelphia, into Maryland, near where the Susquehanna River reaches Chesapeake Bay.]

Appendix 3

Rhode Islanders in Action

Anthony Walker, in *So Few The Brave* (1981), details the organizational structure and experiences of the men from Rhode Island in the Revolutionary War, including information regarding the regimental colors Rhode Islanders carried from 1777 onward. The following is drawn from that book.

During the summer and fall of 1775 the Rhode Island troops and the rest of the American army outside Boston found themselves engaged in housekeeping and training activities. The British (in Boston) remained quietly behind their fortifications. Rhode Island troops were governed by a document containing 53 articles, most of which reappeared as regulations for the Continental forces. "No striking a superior officer; No desertion allowed; No duels permitted; No more than 39 stripes (lashes) to be awarded for any one offense" and so on. When, in September, Washington directed that a special force of 1100 men be formed from volunteers willing to follow Colonel Benedict Arnold in a march through the Maine wilderness to the walls of Quebec city, some of the best soldiers in the army came forward to join this hazardous enterprise. In addition to four officers, Rhode Island provided about 100 men. The expedition moved out of Cambridge on 15 September, heading north toward the Maine woods and their confrontation with adversity which others have chronicled.

In 1776, the enlistment period was for one year, and for many men it was expiring. Washington was faced with a situation of reorganizing the Continentals and reenlisting as many men as possible for the coming year. Rhode Island's contribution in 1776 was two regiments of 600 men each, formed as the 9th and 11th Continentals. There is no record of what colors these two regiments flew. They were on watch outside Boston until on 17 March 1776 when the British army boarded transports and abandoned their only foothold in the territory of the United Colonies.

The Americans proceeded to New York City, anticipating that this might be the next goal of the British. Indeed, British ships were sighted off Long Island on 29 June but they made no move to land their troops. In spite of their presence offshore, the Continental army assembled on parade to hear the first reading of the Declaration of Independence. (The Grand Union flag, first flown on Prospect Hill outside Boston was also flown on Long Island, according to a British observer.)

Washington's forces were divided between Manhattan and Long Island, when on Thursday August 22 the British commenced their invasion of Long Island from Staten Island. They landed to the rear of the American forces and a furious battle followed on August 27, in which more than 1000 Americans were captured, wounded or killed. The Americans fell back to the defenses of Brooklyn Heights, which the British under General William Howe elected not to attack. Washington was able to withdraw his forces under cover of night to Manhattan but the news of the defeat was devastating in the colonies.

Hang John Adams

I digress briefly from the story of the Rhode Islanders: David McCullough in his book *John Adams* (2001) provides interesting detail on the defense of New York, and a conference that took place between members of the Continental Congress and Admiral Howe, representing the King, as follows:

At Long Island the British had taken as prisoner General Sullivan, and Admiral Richard Lord Howe chose to release him to carry a message to Congress, which General Sullivan delivered on September 3. Lord Howe requested a meeting to discuss an offer from the King. John Adams, Benjamin Franklin and Edward Rutledge agreed to go to Staten Island to meet with Lord Howe. At the onset, the Admiral observed that all would be better if only he had arrived before the Declaration of Independence was adopted; it had changed the ground. Were it given up, however, he (the Admiral) might possibly "effect the King's purpose ... to restore peace and grant pardons."

Because the Continental Congress had no standing with the Admiral, he would only discuss the situation with the three men as private citizens of some influence. After several hours of discussion, Admiral Howe said at last that if the colonies could not give up "independency" then negotiation was impossible. The war would continue. McCullough states that John Adams would not have been pardoned; he would have been hung on the King's orders.

Getting back to Anthony Walker's book, *So Few The Brave*, he says that when the British ultimately forced Washington and his men back into New Jersey, the Rhode Islanders deported themselves well in various engagements. By 7 December, 1776, the colonial army had fallen back to the Delaware River and crossed over into Pennsylvania opposite Trenton. It was from this base that the discouraged Washington decided to attack. The one year enlistment of many of the men was about to run out and they had suffered nothing but defeats. In three weeks Washington had retreated ninety miles.

The situation was bleak and something dramatic was needed. Washington made a decision to attack across the Delaware on the morning of 26 December 1776, which led to the taking of 918 Hessians who had been comfortably ensconced in the homes and taverns of Trenton. The Rhode Islanders did not take part in this action; they crossed the river on 27 December and occupied Burlington. There were subsequent indecisive actions at Trenton and Princeton before the British withdrew. Washington marched his men over the next three days to winter quarters at Morristown but the victory energized the patriots. [This critical time in the war is exceedingly well covered in *"Washington's Crossing"* (Fischer, 2004).]

At the end of 1776, as at the end of 1775, the short term enlistments of the Continental soldiers expired and Washington had to rebuild his army. This time Congress sought to organize a new militia based on long term service.

It was at this time, in early 1777 that the 1st and 2nd Rhode Island regiments were formed. They were never up to their authorized strength, and in large measure were comprised of the men who had fought in 1775 and 1776. However, in April the two under-strength formations headed out for New Jersey, completing the 200 mile March to Morristown in twelve days. One can well imagine that there was a celebration in Rhode Island as the regiments left, with their silk regimental flags flying in the breeze, the canton with thirteen five-pointed stars arranged 3-2-3-2-3 painted on them.

On 2 July Washington ordered the Rhode Island men to Peekskill to prevent General Howe from going up the Hudson to join up with Burgoyne. Howe made no such move, instead heading for the Delaware River and Philadelphia. On 29 September Washington ordered the Rhode Islanders to join the forces defending Philadelphia. As the men marched toward Philadelphia they learned of the defeat at Brandywine, and when they crossed the Delaware above Trenton they learned that the British firmly occupied Philadelphia. [Some historians say they fought at the battle of the Brandywine which, by this account, is incorrect.] The defensive effort now was to prevent Howe from receiving supplies by water up the Delaware.

Red Bank, New Jersey and Fort Mercer

General Hazelwood of the Pennsylvania Navy was responsible for defending the river, but General Washington was required to provide troops to man the two forts, Mercer and Mifflin, located a few miles downstream from the Quaker city. Mercer was built on the New Jersey side of the Delaware at Red Bank, Mifflin on an island in the stream about 1,900 yards northwest. On 7 October Washington ordered the 1st Rhode Island regiment to march to Red Bank, occupy and defend Fort Mercer. When the 250 men arrived, their Colonel realized they would need more help and asked for the 2nd Rhode Island regiment to be sent. On 19 October, they marched in. On 21 October, the Fort was shelled by British war ships while a force of Hessians organized for a land assault. After several hours of shelling back and forth, the British ships sought to withdraw but in the process the sixty-four gun *Augusta* and the frigate *Merlin* ran aground. Hot shot from the American batteries set both of them on fire and after several minutes they exploded. The naval battle had been won.

Meanwhile, the Hessians, who had been delayed by downed bridges, advanced on the Fort in two columns. They passed through the outer fortifications without interruption and as they converged on the inner redoubt they thought themselves already victorious. Waiting until the German mercenaries had closed to within thirty yards the Rhode Islanders opened fire with muskets and cannon. The Hessians reeled back; their own fire could do little damage to the well protected defenders. Eighty-seven Hessians were buried in the ditch outside the fort the next day; the American losses were one captain and four or five privates killed, with twenty or thirty wounded. While this delayed the British, they were ultimately victorious, reducing the fort to ruins by cannon fire from ships in the river. The passage to Philadelphia was opened just in time for General Howe to receive much needed supplies that he could not get overland because of Washington's forces.

The Rhode Islanders stayed with Washington through the winter at Valley Forge; they were involved in the Battle of Monmouth, and later that summer (1778) they began a campaign on their home ground in Rhode Island to dislodge the British. In this, they were counting on the French fleet, which was blockading Narragansett Bay, to disembark 4000 Marines to launch a simultaneous attack on the British and force their withdrawal from Newport and Rhode Island. Unfortunately, the effort came to naught as the French fleet had been damaged in a storm and could not follow through.

In January 1781, with their numbers depleted, the 1st and 2nd regiments were reorganized into a single force known as Olney's Battalion, which was present at Yorktown. Olney's Battalion was ultimately disbanded in November 1783 after the peace treaty was signed.

One final note about the Rhode Islanders: when the Constitution was drafted and submitted to the various states for ratification, Rhode Island held back for various reasons. The leaders feared being dominated by the large states; they had put fiscal measures into place to clear up their state debt, and they saw themselves as being importers and wholesalers to the other colonies. They could be completely independent and thrive in commerce after the fashion of the Netherlands, attracting business from ports where United States taxes and regulations would make goods more expensive. Secondarily, the Quakers were opposed to a federal government that would countenance slavery. (James, 1975)

However, the new Federal Government was in the process of passing legislation making it illegal for any of the states to do business with Rhode Island if it were independent. This put pressure on Rhode Island, and in May 1790 the General Assembly voted to ratify the Constitution. They were the last state to do so. The new President, George Washington, visited the state in August 1790 *to forgive and embrace the independent state.* On this visit he was welcomed in Newport by, in his own words, *all classes of citizens,* which included the Hebrew Congregation (now the Touro Synagogue) whose Warden, Moses Seixas, wrote him on August 17,

1790, expressing their joy at having a government *"which to bigotry gives no sanction, to persecution no assistance ... but generously affording to all Liberty of conscience, and immunities of Citizenship."*

(The Bill of Rights was being drafted in the Congress and this was important to Rhode Islanders.)

Appendix 4

Rebecca Young

Rebecca Young is part of our story because of a letter her granddaughter wrote in 1875 referencing George Washington's flag, and because her daughter Mary made the flag which flew over Fort McHenry in 1814. Rebecca was a flag maker in Philadelphia, advertising in the *Pennsylvania Packet* in 1781 regarding making "All Kinds of Colours for the Army and Navy". According to the brochure of the Star-Spangled Banner Flag House in Baltimore, Rebecca was widowed during the war and was taken care of by her brother, Benjamin Flower, who was Commissary General of Military Stores under George Washington.

She supported her family of five children by making military supplies, such as musket balls, drum cases, linings for caps, and blankets. A receipt shows that in July, 1781 she was paid for making a "Continental Standard," but there is no record of its design. She made four more in the months that followed. This was at the time that the design for Washington's army flag had been agreed upon, and while there is no record that Rebecca was involved in making the army flag, these few could have been to that design. The material required to make the 100 initially specified flags was not available and had to be ordered from France. It was slow in arriving and the initial order was cut in half. By the time the fifty flags were completed they were not distributed, as the war was over.

Rebecca moved to Baltimore in 1807 with her daughter Mary and set up a flag-making shop. Mary had married an English merchant, John Pickersgill, in Baltimore in 1795 and was widowed in 1805. Living in Baltimore, Mary Pickersgill was commissioned to make what became known as the "Star Spangled Banner" which flew over Fort McHenry. How this was accomplished is remembered by Mary's only surviving daughter, Caroline Pickersgill Purdy, who wrote a letter on September 9,

1876, to Georgianna Armistead Appleton (who owned the old flag) to relate her memories of her mother making the flag.

Text of letter by Caroline Purdy:

"Mrs. Appleton, Dear Madam,

*I have lately seen in the newspapers that the noted flag which flew over Fort McHenry in the bombardment of Baltimore is in your possession and is to be sent to the Centennial. I take the liberty to send you a few particulars about the "Flag." It was made by my mother, Mrs. Mary Pickersgill, and I assisted her. My grandmother, Rebecca Young, made the first flag of the Revolution (under General Washington's direction) and for that reason my mother was selected by Commo. Barney and General Stricker, (family connections), to make this **star spangled banner** [emphasis added] which she did, being an exceedingly patriotic woman.*

The flag being so very large, my mother was obliged to obtain permission from the proprietors of Claggetts brewery which was in our neighborhood to spread it out in their malt house; and I remember seeing my mother down on the floor, placing the stars; after the completion of the flag, she superintended the topping of it, having it fastened in the most secure manner to prevent its being torn away by balls; the wisdom of her precaution was shown during the engagement; many shots piercing it, but it still remained firm to the staff. Your father (Col Armistead) declared that no one but the maker of the flag should mend it, and requested that the rents should be merely bound around.

The flag contained, I think, four hundred yards of bunting, and my mother worked many nights until 12 o'clock to complete it in the given time.

I would also state that many of my ancestors were in the Revolution, my Grandfather William Young was a captain in the war; my uncle, Col. Power, was "Commissary General of Military Stores" and "Colonel of Artillery". These both lost their lives by camp fever. I had another uncle taken prisoner by the British and whipped through the fleet for attempting to escape; and my father-in-law, Henry Purdy, served through the war.

For my character and position I could refer you to Miss Margaret Purviance or any other reference you would require; I could further recall myself to your recollection, as I was a manager of the "Aged Woman's Home" at the same time you were, and was particularly associated with you (both being Episcopalians) in the care of a Mrs. Jefferson, daughter of Mr. Whipple, a signer of the Declaration of Independence. Your kindness and prompt attention to her induced me to present my case to you.

I am widowed and childless, and now find myself, in my seventy-sixth year, in feeble health and with the barest pittance of support. My friends here in Balto. have suggested that if those particulars meet with your approbation, and were placed on a card attached to the flag, they might excite among patriotic people some compassion for my helpless condition, but I would leave this matter entirely to your judgment.

I have not been able to write, on account of not having the use of my right arm, but thought it was better to put the signature in my own hand with kind regards. I trust your sympathy.

(Signed) *C. Purdy* (full name Caroline Purdy), *September 9, 1876*

Note that in this letter, she asserted that her grandmother, Rebecca Young, made the first flag of the Revolution "under General Washington's direction." This letter is probably as equally valid for historical purposes as the testimonies of Betsy's descendants. However, it can be interpreted several ways, one of which would fit into the Betsy story as told by Rachel Fletcher, that the 'committee' invited several other flag makers to make sample flags and Betsy's was chosen.

Another possibility is that she is writing about the "continental standard" (design unknown) produced by her grandmother Rebecca Young on July 9, 1781, and that this was the flag for the Army, long awaited by Washington. Rebecca made a small number of them after the initial flag was made. This was at the time that the records show there had been agreement reached as to the design for the Army flag. However, full production of the flag was of necessity delayed pending the arrival from France of the needed materials.

With respect to the information in the letter from Mrs. Purdy, it is the position of the Star Spangled Banner Flag House in Baltimore that she is referring to the Grand Union flag flown by Washington in Massachusetts on January 1, 1776, and that this is the first flag of the Revolution.

Appendix 5

Charles Willson Peale's Diary

In early October word was received in Philadelphia of Washington's losses in New York, and the Philadelphia Associates (militia) met to organize themselves for whatever demands might be put upon them. Peale was elected a second lieutenant; military affairs were conducted in a democratic manner. At a meeting of November 19, he was advanced to first lieutenant. Washington warned congress of a battle for the defense of Philadelphia, which threw the city into a panic. The city troops departed Philadelphia on the fifth of December 1776 for Trenton. Almost immediately they received orders to embark for the Pennsylvania side of the river, where we pick up Peale's diary of action after the first battle of Trenton.

The following is abstracted from: *Charles Willson Peale* by C. C. Sellers (pp. 131-136).

C. W. Peale Diary:

[January 2, 1777.] At one O'clock this morning began a march for Trent Town. The Roads are very muddy, almost over our Shoe Tops. The Number of Troops and Badness of the Way, so many runs to cross and fences to remove makes it a very tedious march. The sun had risen more than an hour before we Reached the Town. Afterwards the difficulty of getting quarters kept us a long time under arms. At last we were provided and had made a fire. I took a short nap on a plank with my feet to the fire. I was suddenly awakened by a Call to Arms, that the Enemy was advancing, and at a small distance from the Town. We soon paraded and joined the Battn: and appeared on the Alarm Ground, where I was greatly struck with the appearance of so fine an army. 4 Brigades at least paraded in the same field below the Town. Soon we heard the Cannon at some distance. We were then ordered to march into a Road through the woods turning downwards. A message

from the General ordered us to return to defend a Road which let into the field w[h]ere we first paraded. When we had marched to this Road, we then wheeled to [the] Right into a wheat Field joining the said Road, where we halled some Cannon and formed in a diagonal manner across part of the field, convenient for the whole to act, should the Enemy appear. After remaining some time in this order we Retired a little back to an Orchard which joined this field, & ground our arms and made fires of the fences. In this time the fireing continued and seem'd to approach nearer.

We now was ordered to take our arms. The Sun appeared to be hardly ½ hour high. We then marched in Platoons back towards the Town, or rather our Alarm Ground. Platoon firing was now perty frequent. When we had almost got out of the Woods . . . word was brought that the Enemy gave way, which at different times was the case. However, they had no[w] got possession of the greatest part of the Town. A very [heavy] firing was kept up on the Bridge, and great numbers of the Enemy fell there. Some of our Artilery stood their ground till the Enemy advanced within 40 Yds. And they was very near loosing the Field Piece. We were now in the field below the Town, and one of our Cannon & a Howett[z]er played on the Town. It was now perty dark, or quite so, before the firing had entirely ceased. Some unlucky shot from a Cannon killed 1 or 2 men of the 3d Battn. of Pha. Troops, Likewise about the same number of Cumberland County Militia. We now marched to the Skirts of the field and grounded our arms & sett to making fires out of the fence Rails, & Talk over the fatigues of the Day, and soon after Eating Laid themselves down to Sleep. Captn. Bernie joined us just before we had the alarm & marched with us during the Day, tho' his Legg, which he had hurt some time ago, would not permit him to march with us from Crosswicks. He now complains that he could not hold out, and desired me to take charge of the Company. He told General Cadwallader that he was not able to serve. We took out some of you Baggage from the wagon & sent it away and at 12 [midnight] was ordered to parade. By the sending away [of] the wagons & our parading at this hour, I realy expected a Retreat.

One gathers from Peale's journal that the militia seemed to believe almost every movement of the army to be a retreat. They were not confident of victory, nor could one expect them to be. It is not to the discredit of these good fellows that they had turned out in the first place to join a beaten army for what all the city believed to be the end of a lost campaign, and then bore as steadily as they did the winter weather and the long, exhausting marches. In this war the militia were rarely honored with posts of danger. Their part so far had been a secondary one. But now, by a *ruse de guerre* and a surprise thrust, Washington was about to win back almost the whole of New Jersey in a single battle and, by chance and mischance, the city battalions would bear the brunt of it. As for Peale, he now commanded his company, a promotion that would be confirmed in his captain's commission of June 17, 1777.

Leaving a few men ostentatiously digging trenches by the light of large campfires, by midnight Washington had his entire army on the march to Princeton, making a wide detour to the east to avoid detection. Though muddy by day, now the road was frozen hard, and the column moved steadily onward through the dark hours until the first slow red light of dawn brought into view around them earth and silent houses and masses of twig and branches of bare trees, all crystalline with frozen dew. They were at Princeton, but just too late to take their enemy wholly by surprise. Mawhood's brigade of three regiments had already broken camp to join Cornwallis and was advancing upon them.

General Hugh Mercer's Continentals came first into action to be met by a fierce bayonet charge. Having themselves no bayonets, they fled ingloriously, leaving their General mortally wounded behind them. By the fortune of war, Cadwalader's command was now closest to the scene of action. The Commander in Chief himself led them on. The New Englanders formed first, the militia following their example. The battle began again. Peale deployed his men with the rest and, though he judged the fight not yet close enough, hurled with the rest a volley into the advancing enemy. They were soon at closer quarters. The attack which had routed the Continentals was threatening to break the reserve as well. Where the shock bore heaviest, Washington rode out in front and his wavering battle line steadied and held behind him.

The charge of the British halted and they opened fire. But for some reason their shots flew high, while the untried Philadelphians poured in deadly volley after volley, advancing to fire, stepping back to load, advancing to fire again. The artillery of both sides added a thunderous bellowing to the bursts of musketry, and again, the brown-clad townsmen excelled their professional opponents, tearing the scarlet ranks before them with their iron. Washington rallied Mercer's men and brought new regiments into action, lengthening and advancing his whole line. A few minutes more, then suddenly the British were throwing down their arms, abandoning their cannon, running back in confusion toward where the college buildings loomed up on the hill beyond.

Far on the right of the city troops, an officer roared, *"Huzzah!"* shouting, *"They fly! The day is our own!"* and the cheer rolled like a wave along the line.

Diary:

. . .I realy expected a Retreat.

[January] 3d. At one Oclock in the morning we began to move, and directed our Course through the Woods directly from the River and after some time more northerly. By this I expected we were going to surround the Enemy, but after marching some miles I learnt I was going a Bye Road to [Princeton]. We were marched perty fast. However, the Sun had risen just before we See Prinstown. We proceeded as fast as possible and was within a mile of the Town when we were informed that all was quiet. A short time after, the Battn. just ahead of us began a Exceeding quick Platoon firing and some Cannon. We marched on quick an met some of the Troops retreating in confusion. We continued our march towards the Hill w[h]ere the firing was, tho' now rather irregularly. I carried my Platoon to the Top of the Hill & fired, tho' very unwillingly, for I thought the Enemy rather too far off, and then retreated. Loading. We Returned to the charge, & fired a 2nd time & Retreated as before. The 3rd time coming up, the Enemy began to Retreat. I must here give the New England Troops their due. They were the first who regularly formed . . . & stood the fire without regarding [the] Balls which whistled their thousand different notes around our heads, and what is very astonishing did little or no harm: none that I know of where we were. Some that had retreated and then advanced through a Wood on our right engaged the Enemy. We lost in all about 12 men. Genl. Mercer was wounded in his Leg and fell into the Enemys Hands when our men was first surprised, and when they in turn was obliged to give way, they stabed him with a Bayonet. We lost, besides, Captn. Shippen of 2 Battn & [a] Lieutenant in the 1st. Batn. of Pha. Militia.

We now advanced towards the Town, & halted at about ¼ of a mile distance till the Artilery came up and our men were collected in better order. Amediately on the Artilery firing, a Number [of the enemy] that had formed near the College began to disperse, and amediately a Flag was sent, and we huzared Victory.

Before them the field was strewn with fallen men, discarded weapons and baggage. Prisoners were being herded together and marched away. You can glimpse the scenes as Peale has painted them in the backgrounds of his full-length *Washingtons*: the Americans dashing forward under a blue banner with a circle of thirteen stars, the bleak meadow below the college buildings, the red-coated captives guarded by men in buff and blue.

A few days later, Dr. Benjamin Rush was echoing Peale's praise of the New England men while glowing with pride for what his own compatriots had done. "The Philadelphia militia behaved like heroes." So they had. It was a triumph for the militia service, due in part, of course, to the fact that these burghers had lived together and drilled together and had become a more coherent force than the country levies were ever likely to be.

After the huzzahs of victory died away, the soldiers, resting on their arms, awaited eagerly the order to advance into the town for rest and food. This comfortable prospect was broken by a rumble of cannon in their rear. At first they thought it must come from Trenton, but soon found it not only to be nearer, but rapidly approaching. Cornwallis' rear, at Maidenhead, had now become his vanguard and was pushing forward against them. The order to march again was shouted through the army. The weary battalions moved up the hill and through the town and, without stopping, pushed onward toward the north. It seemed again like a retreat, with the enemy hard at their heels. But Washington had it in mind to strike at New Brunswick, Cornwallis' base of supplies, a bold stroke that might, he thought, end the war. His generals dissuaded him from it, for the exhausted army was all but asleep upon its feet.

By midday the roads had become again a sea of mud. A wrong turn was taken and halt cried along the files. Some, thinking that this meant a skirmish with the light horse who rode in the British advance, fixed their bayonets. Others, among them many of Peale's company, merely sat down upon the wet and barren earth and declared that they could no longer either march or fight. He reasoned with them as best he could, but a number had to be left where they were, to follow along behind the army as soon as they were able. Later in the day, he halted his company by a bridge and there collected a few of the stragglers.

Diary:

I then marched off and continued our way perty briskly and got to Somerset Court House, and expected to have quarters in the Court House, as [I] was told [by] some of the men [to whom] I applied, but found it was occupied by the Prisoners, and then I pushed on to a Tavern a little further, and got them into the Loft amongst a fine heap of straw, where some Hessians had lay'd. This was gladly excepted by them, who was at other Places very dainty: they would not go into a House where the Soldiers had been quartered for fear of their Lice. Now they layed down and most of [them] was asleep in a few moments so sound that I could not get a single man to go with me to get Provisions. I had the Promise of [a] barrel of Flower of Coll. Cox, and had the lent of a Oven, but could get nobody to assist me in bringing it to be Bak'd. I then went to a House farther in Town & purchased some Beef, which I got the good Woman to boil against I should call for it in the morning. And I got a small kettle full of Petatoes Boil'd where we lodged. I then layed me down to rest amongst the men on the Hessian Straw and thought myself happy, tho' the Room was as full of Smoak as if to cure Bacon. Some New England Troops had made a fire in an old Chimney that let almost all the smoak amongst us. However, by covering our heads in our blankets... we lay rested quiet for the night.

Peale was a thin, spare, pale-faced man, in appearance totally unfit to endure the fatigues of long marches, and lying on the cold wet ground, sometimes covered with snow. Yet by temperance and by a forethought of providing for the worst that might happen, he endured this campaign better than many others whose appearance was more robust. He always carried a piece of dryed Beef and Bisquits in his Pocket, and Water in his Canteen, which, he found, was much better than Rum.

Appendix 6

Captain Edward Williams

According to Randy W. Hackenburg (1992): "The Cameron Guards were recruited and organized by Captain Edward C. Williams in Harrisburg specifically for service in the Mexican War. They were named for Senator Simon Cameron. Through close contacts with political and military leaders in the state, Captain Williams was able to have the Guards accepted to serve with the 2nd Regiment." They were mustered into federal service in Pittsburg on 2 January 1847. They saw action in the battles of La Hoya, Chapultepec and Garita de Belen. With the end of the war, they were mustered out at Pittsburg on 20 July 1848. Of 97 men who served in the company, 21 Guards died in service and an additional sixteen received discharges before muster out.

In the folklore about this Company, we have it that a report was filed on September 15, 1847 by Major William Brindle about the action at Chapultepec, in which Captain Williams is said to have raised the Stars and Strips over the Fort after the surrender of the Mexican General in command. None of the action reports filed by officers of the volunteer companies were made part of official army files. Some were published in the *Pennsylvanian* (Philadelphia) but the report by Major Brindle was not among them.

In 1899, with the Betsy Ross story in its ascendancy, Major Brindle recalled the report he had filed about Capt. Edward Williams after the Chapultepec battle because of its connection to Betsy Ross. He wrote the Secretary of War to inquire about his report. He filed a duplicate, but we do not know what happened to the duplicate. The only source of Major Brindle's report is in a publication of *The Snyder County Historical Society, Bulletin II*, No. 4, pp. 504-505. The date of this issue is 1941-1942. It is a compilation of presentations at the regular monthly meetings of the Society. The May 1942 meeting had a presentation by Dewey S. Herrold on Brigadier-General Edward Charles Williams, and that is the source of the Major Brindle report on the battle in Randy Hackenburg's book. A significant piece of history relevant to Betsy Ross, almost lost, has been recovered.

```
The Second Pennsylvania Regiment
Second Brigade, Volunteer Division
In the Valley of Mexico, September 12, 13, and 14, 1847
Report of Major Commanding

Letter of Transmittal
No 1519 W. Street, N. W.,
Washington, D.C.
June 15, 1899.

Hon. R. A. Alger,
Secretary of War,
Sir:

     Upon inquiry in your Department, I learned that
my report of the part taken by the Second Pennsylvania
Regiment, composed of an extra number of companies, which
served as the Second Brigade of Major General John A.
Quitman's "volunteer division", in the contest with the
Mexicans in the Valley of Mexico on the 12, 13, and 14 of
Sept. 15, 1847 to Lieut. Col. John W. Geary to be handed into
Division Headquarters, with his report. It cannot be found
on file in your Department. It was destroyed or suppressed,
as I am informed. In justice to the gallant Pennsylvanians
who served in the Second Pennsylvania Regiment, I herewith
file in your Department a duplicate copy of my report.

                    I am, very respectfully,
                      Your obedient servant,


                      Wm. Brindle
                      Late Major and Lieutenant-Colonel
                      Second Pennsylvania Regiment
```

What we have today is his story as he told it then, because he kept a copy. The *Action Report* is to be found in Randy Hackenburg's book (1992) and his source is a presentation to The Snyder County Historical Society in 1942 by Dewey S. Herrold. Herrold describes the wartime experience of the Cameron Guards, from the time they organized in Harrisburg until their mustering out. The Major Brindle report is specific in stating that Captain Williams brought a Betsy Ross from the State Library in Harrisburg, and this is the flag that was flown over the Fort.

Brindle's Report of 15 September

Head-Quarters, Second Brigade, Vol. Division.
Citadel, City of Mexico, September 15, 1847.

Shortly before daybreak on the 13th instant Lieut. Richard Hammond, an aide of General Shields, conveyed an order to me for the General of the Division to join the Second Pennsylvania Regiment at Battery No.1, near Tacubaya, with my command to participate in an assault upon the Fortress Chapultepec.... On the meadows, and under my eye, Captain E. C. Williams, of Company G "Cameron Guards" of Harrisburg, Pa., was struck by a ball, near the top of the shoulder, high enough to turn the shoulder. It threw him forward on his hands and knees, severely wounded. He was quickly on his feet again, and continued on duty with his company until the fighting was concluded in the City of Mexico. Had the ball struck his shoulder slightly lower it would have been a mortal wound.... As soon as the Second Pennsylvania Regiment had passed the wall of the Fortress, it encountered its garrison, about 800 strong, composed of artillery and infantry, which we drove back to the arch on the front of the Fortress, and under it where it surrendered.

I placed a guard over the prisoners, and then hastened to the eastern end of the Fortress, where I met the aged General Bravo, its commander, who stood with his arms folded over his chest, in the attitude of surrender. He was an ex-President of Mexico, and had fought gallantly to make it independent of Spain. I did not deem it necessary to humiliate him by taking his sword. At this moment General Quitman came up the roadway leading into the Fortress on the southeast. I met him and turned over to him the Fortress and the prisoners the Second Pennsylvania Regiment had taken in it. He directed me to have the Second Pennsylvania Regiment replenish its ammunition and proceed to the attack on the Garita-de-Belen, about two miles from the Fortress. At the moment when I met General Bravo, Lieutenant Charles B. Bowers, of Captain Gallagher's company of (F) the New York Regiment, then serving with Battery No. 2, approached. Apparently he had been separated from his company and regiment; and attempted to assault General Bravo with his sword. I ordered him to halt, and called his attention to the fact that General Bravo, with his arms folded over his chest had surrendered, and ordered Bowers to put up his sword.... Captain E. C. Williams, of Company G, Second Pennsylvania Regiment soon after we entered the Fortress, ascended to the top of it, with the first American Flag made by Betsy Ross, of Philadelphia, which was presented to General Washington just before the battle of Trenton, during the Revolution of 1776, which Captain Williams had obtained from the State Library at Harrisburg, Pa., and carried with him to Mexico, with the purpose of raising it over the enemy's works at every opportunity, and which he raised over the Fortress of Chapultepec about the same time that a sergeant of one of the old infantry regiments raised a blue regimental flag over it. To Captain Williams belongs the honor of having raised the first American Flag over the Fortress.... Shortly before daylight on the 14th instant an Englishman who owned and operated a cotton factory, near the Citadel, whose property would have been destroyed if the batteries had opened fire, came running with a white flag to the General of the Division, who was about to open fire with the batteries, and informed him that General Santa Anna had marched out of the city by the Northeast Gate with his army. The General put the bearer of the white flag in my charge, to hold him with us until we ascertained whether his information was true or false. The General immediately ordered his command "forward". We found the battery at the Southeast of the Citadel abandoned, and also the Citadel, when I released the bearer of the white flag, with thanks. The Second Pennsylvania Regiment was placed as a garrison in the Citadel, when Captain E. C. Williams ran up over it that American Flag which he had so proudly raised over the Fortress. To Captain Williams also belongs the honor of having raised the First American Flag over any public building in the city of Mexico.... I cannot conclude my report without expressing my admiration of the good conduct and gallantry of every officer and man of the Second Pennsylvania Volunteer Regiment. I also express my thanks to them for the splendid and regular order in which they charged up the hill and into the Fortress which elicited the applause of all who witnessed their charge. The Second Pennsylvania Regiment lost eight killed, and eighty-nine wounded. A detailed list of the killed and wounded will accompany the report of Lieutenant Colonel Geary.

I am, very respectfully, Your obedient servant,

William Brindle, Major Commanding

Second Brigade, Volunteer Division

A column on Captain Edward Williams was printed in *Harpers Weekly* on July 27, 1861, page 466, which describes his raising a stars and strips over Chapeltepec, but it doesn't speak of the source of the flag. We only learn that from the action report of Major Brindle, and from the interview with Captain Williams printed in the *Harrisburg-Telegraph* on Saturday, February 29, 1896. The same story is carried in his obituary in *The Middleburgh Post* (Snyder County, Pennsylvania) Thursday Feb. 22, 1900.

The flag at the heart of the story was taken from the State Library to decorate the hall when the Cameron Guards were being feted before they set off to war. Captain Williams took the flag with him, knowing the story that it was the Betsy Ross flag, commonly known as the "Trenton" flag given to George Washington by Betsy before that battle. It may be folklore, but this is what Major Brindle wrote the day after the battle.

One fact that is certain is that Edward Williams was born in Philadelphia in 1820 and moved to Harrisburg when he was eighteen. As a teenager, he would have known of folklore about Betsy at about the time of the 50th anniversary of the Revolution and the Declaration of Independence. And he did carry a stars and stripes flag with him, to be flown when appropriate.

HARPER'S WEEKLY.

A JOURNAL OF CIVILIZATION

VOL. V.—No. 239.]   NEW YORK, SATURDAY, JULY 27, 1861.   [SINGLE COPIES SIX CENTS.
[$2 50 PER YEAR IN ADVANCE.

Entered according to Act of Congress, in the Year 1861, by Harper & Brothers, in the Clerk's Office of the District Court for the Southern District of New York.

BRIGADIER GENERAL WILLIAMS.—FROM A PHOTOGRAPH.—[SEE NEXT PAGE.]

Reprint of the *Harper Weekly* column

GEN. EDWARD C. WILLIAMS.

GENERAL EDWARD C. WILLIAMS, whose portrait we give on the preceding page, was born on the 10th of February, 1820, in the city of Philadelphia, where he resided until the year 1838. In the spring of 1838, being then but a youth of 18 years, he removed to the city of Harrisburg, there to commence the journey of life. Upon his arrival he at once found employment in the book-bindery of the Messrs. Canteens. Here he remained for some time. Quiet and industrious in manner, he became extremely useful to his employers.

But the quiet of life was not compatible with his disposition. In December, 1846, he left the city of Harrisburg in command of the Cameron Guards, Second Regiment Pennsylvania Volunteers, to join our army, then in Mexico. At the head of his company he took an active part in the capture of Vera Cruz, thence through the different battles which took place upon the lines of our veteran Commander-in-chief. Being wounded at Chapultepec, in the hottest of the fight, he did not leave his command, but bravely led them to the taking of the castle, upon the top of which, with his own hand, he hoisted the stars and stripes. Again, at the city of Mexico, his hand was the first to grasp the halliards to which was attached the first American flag that floated over the Mexican capital. At the close of the war he returned to the city of Harrisburg, since which time he has filled different offices of trust with credit to himself and his constituents. At the breaking out of the war we find him among the first to offer his sword for the preservation of our Union.

General Williams was married in the year 1841 to Miss Hetzel, of Harrisburg. Three brothers of this lady served with distinction through the entire Mexican war. A nephew of General Williams, just graduated at the Military Academy at West Point, is now serving his country in the city of Washington, being a second lieutenant in the First Artillery. Another nephew is still at West Point. Since the rebellion General Williams has been constantly engaged with his many duties.

Timeline

Significant Dates in the Evolution of Our National Flag, and Related Events in Our National History

January 1, 1752	Elizabeth Griscom is born on the family farm in New Jersey, the sixth of the nine surviving children of Samuel and Rebecca Griscom.
1756	The Griscom family moves to Philadelphia. Little Betsy is educated in Quaker schools.
c. 1770-1773	Betsy Griscom is apprenticed to John Webster, a London upholsterer who has established a business in Philadelphia.
November 4, 1773	Betsy Griscom marries John Ross.
October 9, 1774	George Washington writes to Captain Robert McKenzie, who had served under him in the French and Indian War, "No such thing [as independence] is desired by any thinking man in America".
April 19, 1775	The Battle of Lexington Green and Concord is fought as the British attempt to seize weapons and supplies.
June 17, 1775	Battle of Bunker (Breeds) Hill is fought.
Late 1775	The Pennsylvania Navy puts floating row gallies into service, flying the Pine Tree Flag, similar to Massachusetts. (Jackson)
January 1, 1776	Washington takes command of the Continental Army at Cambridge. The Grand Union Flag is flown by Washington. Quaife (1942) notes that the change from the existing British flag to the Grand Union flag is simple to visualize and execute, substituting stripes for the solid red body of the flag, and that

thus the change to stars in place of the crosses would be an equally simple and obvious change.

January 21, 1776   John Ross dies, having been cared for by his wife for the preceding eighteen months. He is said to have been engaging in physical activity to keep warm while protecting supplies on the wharf with other volunteers. He fell ill in what was later described as a mental problem. The story of an explosion on the dock was presumably created by someone to hide the facts of the mental illness, a condition that had apparently also afflicted his mother. It has also been suggested that his death may have been a result of poison inhalation.

March 26, 1776   Washington forces the British evacuation of Boston; the British sail to Halifax, Nova Scotia.

May 31, 1776   From Philadelphia, Washington writes to his brother, with respect to the resolution of the Virginia Convention regarding relations with Britain. "Things have now come to such a pass as to convince us that we have nothing more to expect from the justice of Great Britain."

Late May, early June 1776

Washington is in Philadelphia for consultation with the Continental Congress. Betsy Ross is said to have been visited by three men with respect to making a flag: George Washington, her uncle-by-marriage Colonel George Ross (an aide to General Washington), and Robert Morris. Morris is presiding officer of the Pennsylvania Committee of Safety (Jackson). Ross is also a Colonel in the Pennsylvania State Militia. The presence of George Washington, and his lead role in the group, are part of Betsy's story as told by her family members later. The original rough flag drawing which the men brought is re-worked by Washington and a flag is made. Colonel Ross subsequently brings her word that the final product had been approved.

May-June 1776	During this period, Robert Morris is also Chairman of the "Secret Committee" of Congress in Philadelphia. (Later he becomes Chairman of the Continental Congress Marine Committee.)
June 1776	Delegates to the Continental Congress arrive in Philadelphia with instructions to vote for independence.
June 28, 1776	Francis Hopkinson arrives in Philadelphia as a delegate. He is well known in Philadelphia.
July 1, 1776	The British Fleet is off Sandy Hook prior to landing troops on Long Island, and Ambrose Earle, on board Lord Howe's flagship Eagle, wrote to the Earl of Dartmouth, "They have set up their standard in the Fort upon the southern point of Town, the colors are stripes of Red and White alternately with the English Union in the Canton." (Furlong and McCandless, 1981) [The Grand Union flag remains in use after the Declaration of Independence].
July 4, 1776	The Declaration of Independence is adopted, with signatures collected in August including those of two of Betsy's in-laws by marriage.
July 12, 1776	Hopkinson is appointed a member of the Marine Committee.
August 19, 1776	Captain William Richards, Storekeeper, writes the Pennsylvania Committee of Safety as follows: "I hope you have agreed what sort of colors I am to have made for the galley's etc. as they are much wanted." ["I hope you have agreed" strongly suggests that more than one design is being considered. Hopkinson has been in Philadelphia, and on the Marine Committee, long enough to have conceived a flag design for the use of both fleets, which he would likely have actively promoted as a unifying emblem.]
September, 1776	Ben Franklin sails for Paris as Ambassador. (Several years later he writes to the King of the Two Sicilies that our flag has red, white and blue stripes.)

September 26, 1776

> The Continental Marine Committee puts the Continental Navy Captains on the Delaware River under the control of the Pennsylvania Navy Commodore Hazelwood.

October 15, 1776   Captain William Richards again writes regarding colors for the fleet. "The Commodore was with me this morning and says the fleet has not yet any colors to hoist if they should be called on duty. It is not in my power to get them until there is a design fixed on to make the colors by." The argument over the design of a flag continues.

November 18, 1776

> Hopkinson chairs the three-member Continental Navy Board which was formed on this date to coordinate the efforts of the Pennsylvania Navy and Continental armed vessels on the Delaware. The other members are John Nixon and John Wharton.

January 1777   Colonel Benjamin Flower is appointed Commissary General of Military Stores by George Washington. (He is the brother of Rebecca Young, seamstress.)

February 23, 1777 Captain William Richards' store of bunting includes 89 yards of red, 105 yards of white and 166 yards of blue. (Moeller) No mention of the use made of this material.

May 29, 1777   Betsy Ross is paid by the Pennsylvania State Navy Board for delivering ships colors to William Richards storehouse.

June 14, 1777   The Flag Resolution is passed by the Congress, with its description of the "new constellation" of stars. John Adams is Chairman of the Board of War. Barton, in working on a Great Seal design in 1782, describes the "new constellation" as a circle of stars depicting perpetuity, and continuity. [Johnson (1930) suggests that "the new flag was already public knowledge and the lack of public records, criticism or comment, paradoxical as it may seem, is itself a record of a peculiarly convincing kind." In other words, the design with its circle of stars feature had been shown around and discussed.]

June 14, 1777	At the same meeting, John Paul Jones is put in command of the Ranger, under construction in Portsmouth, New Hampshire.
June 15, 1777	The widow Betsy Ross marries Joseph Ashburn, by coincidence the day after the Flag Resolution is passed.
July 4, 1777	The City of Philadelphia celebrates the first anniversary of the Declaration of Independence. The next day, July 5th, John Adams writes to his daughter, Abigail, in great detail describing the excitement and colorful nature of the celebration, but with no mention of our nation's flag being flown.
July 8, 1777	The Pennsylvania Packet publishes a full account of a celebration of the first anniversary of the Declaration of Independence. According to this account, everybody of importance is involved in the day long event. The Hessian Band captured at Trenton the previous Christmas supplies music for the occasion. "About noon, as the celebration got under way, all the armed ships and gallies in the river were drawn up before the city, dressed in gayest manner, with the colours of the United States and streamers flying."
September 2, 1777	The Flag Resolution is published in the Pennsylvania Packet, and the next day in the Pennsylvania Gazette (Quaife, 1942).
October 17, 1777	Burgoyne surrenders at Saratoga. A stars and stripes flag is carried in battle at Ticonderoga, June 30, 1777, according to the diary of a British Lieutenant, William Digby.
November 1, 1777	John Paul Jones sails from Portsmouth, New Hampshire in the Ranger for France to convey the news of Burgoyne's surrender in mid-October to our representatives in Paris.
November 1777	John Adams leaves Philadelphia for Braintree, Massachusetts, to prepare to go to France, having been appointed by Congress to replace Deane as one of the joint Commissioners in Paris.

November 16, 1777
Fort Mifflin (in the Delaware) falls; British take down the American Flag; contemporary drawings show the stars in lines. (Jackson)

November 1777
The British occupy Philadelphia; the Continental Congress relocates to Baltimore, and then to York, Pennsylvania.

December 2, 1777
John Paul Jones arrives at Nantes, France. News of Burgoyne's surrender had already reached France by another ship, the Penet. Time is spent re-rigging and putting new sails on the Ranger to make her a better ship. Jones goes to Paris on December 15th.

January 16, 1778
Jones receives orders to equip the Ranger "in the best manner for the cruise you propose" which Jones sees as an opportunity to harass the British on land and sea. The cruise for that purpose begins February 13, 1778.

February 13, 1778
John Adams boards the frigate Boston at Braintree, but because of a storm and the presence of British ships they are unable to sail until February 19th. The crossing is very rough.

February 14, 1778
Jones receives a salute to the Stars and Stripes from the Admiral of the French Fleet in Quiberon Bay, before departing on his raids on shipping and on the British Isles.

February 24, 1778
According to a letter home by John Adams, the frigate Boston, while en route to France, seeking a prize, chases a Sail, firing a gun to leeward and hoisting the American Colours; the ship they are chasing hoists the French Colours of the Province of Normandy. The prevailing wind makes it impossible for the ships to come about and speak. The "colours" are not described.

February 1778
Rebecca Young's husband dies, she and her children are taken in by her brother Colonel Benjamin Flower. [Rebecca Young is in the Timeline because she had connections to the Quartermaster of the Continental Army, whereas Betsy's connections were to the Pennsylvania Committee of Safety. Rebecca is given the order to

make the "Continental Standard" at about the time the design of the flag for the Army is finalized.]

April 1, 1778   The frigate Boston arrives at Bordeaux with John Adams; he reaches Paris on April 8th.

April 24, 1778   The Ranger engages H.M.S. Drake and takes it as a prize, jury-rigs sails and puts a crew on board.

April 1778   Hopkinson's 40 dollar note is printed. It has a circle of stars with the all-seeing eye of Providence; the stars have eight points.

May 8, 1778   The Ranger and Drake enter Brest. John Paul Jones gives up command of Ranger, anticipating a larger ship which does not immediately materialize.

May 1778 to February 1779

Jones is "put off again and again about getting a new command" (Morison) and spends the time in Paris with our representatives there.

June 1778   The British withdraw from Philadelphia for New York.

July 1778   Hopkinson resigns from the Continental Navy Board to accept position of Treasurer of Loans.

August 31, 1778   Rebecca Young is paid for 500 musket balls.

September 19, 1778

Rebecca Young is paid for 500 cartridges.

September 26, 1778

Congress authorizes new currency, a large portion of which is issued in January 14, 1779. Hopkinson does the $50 and $60 denominations with new emblems and new border cuts.

October 9, 1778   Franklin (in Paris) writes to the King of the Two Sicilies in describing our naval flag as having red, white and blue stripes in it with 13 white stars in the blue canton. This flag is later flown by John Paul Jones on the Bonhomme Richard. Jones is in Paris at this time.

1778 (late) War Office adopts a seal for official business. It appears on commissions as early as January 7, 1779. The seal contains portions of two flags, one of unidentified design with cord and tassels which could represent a regimental flag, the other a national color of the Revolutionary War period, with cords and tassels. Six stars in two rows of three are seen in the visible part of the canton. Not all the stripes are visible. The seal continues to be used today to authenticate "official" documents.

January 1779 Elizabeth Ashburn (a.k.a. Betsy Ross) is paid for making 500 musket balls.

January 14, 1779 Congress authorizes (by seven separate resolutions passed between January 14 and November 29, 1779) a currency issue including $35, $45, $70 and $80 denominations which were designed by Francis Hopkinson with new emblems and mottos.

February 1779 John Paul Jones is given an old French East Indiaman vessel which he renames the Bonhomme Richard in a compliment to Benjamin Franklin, author of Poor Richard's Almanac, (Morison) and he outfits it for naval use.

May 10, 1779 Richard Peters of the War Board writes to Washington that "as to the colors, we have refused them for another reason. The Baron Von Steuben mentioned that he would settle with your excellency some plan as to the colors—one the Standard of the United States, which would be the same throughout the army and the other a Regimental color, —of the U. States." But it is not yet settled what is the Standard. [Washington's failure to mention having a flag made by Betsy suggests he had another use for that flag.]

June 12, 1779 The Bonhomme Richard, accompanied by Alliance (which had brought Lafayette home to France) and several French ships as a squadron, sails under Jones.

July 1779	Francis Hopkinson, while serving as Treasurer of Loans, becomes Judge of Admiralty for Pennsylvania, a position he held until 1789 when the Admiralty Court was abolished; he is then appointed Judge of the United States Court of the eastern district of Pennsylvania by Washington.
July 14, 1779	Colonel George Ross, Betsy's uncle-by-marriage, dies.
September 3, 1779	Richard Peters writes to Washington with drafts of an army standard for his "approbation, rejection, or alteration." He adds "The one with the Union and Emblem in the middle is preferred by us as being a variant from the marine Flag." Peter's letter disclosed that the Board of War desired an entirely different banner for the Continental Army than the marine flag (which presumably is the stars and stripes).
September 18, 1779	The Pennsylvania State Flag is adopted by the Pennsylvania State Legislature. It is a blue flag "with the arms of the State worked thereon." (Moeller, NAVA News 35/1)
September 23, 1779	Jones and the Bonhomme Richard engage H.M.S. Serapis off Flamborough Head, England; both ships are badly damaged but the victory goes to Jones who is forced to transfer to the captured Serapis. The Serapis and Alliance sail into the harbor of Texel, Holland.
October 4-5, 1779	John Paul Jones' Stars and Stripes are painted while his ships are in the Texel (Holland) harbor. The Serapis flag has thirteen red, white and blue stripes in an irregular sequence and a blue canton with thirteen eight-pointed stars in a 4-5-4 arrangement. The Alliance has seven white and six red stripes with a small blue canton and thirteen eight-pointed stars in a 3-2-3-2-3 pattern. (Richardson, page 28) (Quaife page 43) [The introduction into this timeline of events in the career of John Paul Jones is intended to draw attention to the potential he had for influencing

European views of the design of our early naval and national flag. He spent many months in Paris (Morison 1957) with our envoys there, and sailed on the Bonhomme Richard with a flag of a different design from the one flown on the Alliance, which had just recently left the states. Even the Alliance flag was different from the specifications of the Flag Resolution in that it had a white stripe at the top and on the bottom.]

January 28, 1780   Board of War to Washington: "Sir,... As many colours as possible shall be provided but until we receive the Articles from France, of which we have lately had agreeable Accounts, we cannot have the Standards prepared agreeably to the plan proposed viz: to have two for every Regiment—one, the Standard of the United States, the other, the Regimental Standard,... The Regiments must shift with what Colours can now be given them until the Arrival of our expected Supplies." [A national army standard appears to have been agreed upon.]

March 25, 1780   Hopkinson (now Treasurer of Loans) is employed as a consultant to the second Great Seal committee established to review the work of the first committee and propose a design for the Great Seal. The committee's report is submitted May 10, 1780. The report is referred back to the committee on May 17, 1780.

May 1780   Hopkinson submits first bill for artistic services rendered to the Board of Admiralty, just days after completing his design work on the Great Seal. He writes to the Board, "Gentlemen: It is with great pleasure I understand my last device of a seal for the Board of Admiralty has met with your Honours' approbation. I have with great readiness upon several occasions exerted my small abilities in this way for the public service, as I flatter myself, to the satisfaction of those I wish to please, viz., The flag of the United States of America, 4 devices for the Continental currency, A seal for the Board of Treasury, Ornaments, Devices, and Checks, for the new bills of exchange on Spain and Holland. A seal for Ship Papers of the United States, A Seal for the Board of Admiralty,

The Borders, Ornaments & Checks for the new Continental Currency now in the press, a work of considerable length. A Great Seal for the United States of America, with a Reverse.... For these services I have as yet made no charge nor received any compensation. I now submit it to your Honours' consideration whether a quarter cask of the public wine will not be a proper and a reasonable reward for these labors of fancy and a suitable encouragement to future exertions of the like nature." [National Geographic] [Note: no claim is made by Hopkinson that his flag design was accepted.]

May 25, 1780	Hopkinson's letter is forwarded to the President of Congress. Hopkinson is instructed to "state his account and leave it with the Auditor." He resubmits the bill. The flag is now called "The great Naval Flag of the United States."
May 26, 1780	Rebecca Young is paid for cutting out and making shirts for Colonel Benjamin Flowers, Military Stores Department.
June 24, 1780	Hopkinson is unable to submit vouchers showing he was commissioned to make the designs, but furnishes an itemized account.
June 1780	Immediately after submitting this account, he submits a substitute to alter the basis on which the charges are made to conform to the expectations of the Board as to the basis of exchange. The revised bill now asks: "9.0.0 pounds for The Naval Flag of the United States" and "10.0.0 for the Great Seal of the States with a Reverse, and 5.0.0 for the new currency in press." [Hastings (1939) is willing to recognize Hopkinson's contribution of the design of a flag, because the claim he made for compensation was not refuted by others who would have been aware of his artistic endeavors and would have known better (i.e. questioned it). The statement of his detractors that "others were also involved in the design and artistic work for which he wanted payment" would certainly apply to his work on the Great Seal, but

would it apply to the flag design which was several years earlier, when he was not on the payroll as Treasurer of Loans? Hopkinson asks almost as much for his flag design as he does for his work on the Great Seal.]

August 7, 1780   Money is placed in Rebecca Young's account along with a long list of fabrics and bedding, goods received from Colonel Pickering.

November, 1780   Rebecca Young (various entries) is paid for making blankets.

April 24, 1781   Samuel Wetherill, Junior, as Clerk, issues an open invitation "To Those of the People called Quakers, who have been disowned for Matters Religious or Civil" to join himself and others in the formation of the Society of Free Quakers.

April 28, 1781   Colonel Benjamin Flower dies of tuberculosis ('camp fever').

July 1781   Hopkinson resigns as Treasurer of Loans after a quarrel with the Board of Treasury.

July 14, 1781   Rebecca Young is paid for making a "Continental Standard" for military stores. This is the first payment recorded to her for making a "Continental Standard" which presumably is a flag. [The Army flag Washington has been waiting for?]

July-August-September 1781

Three additional entries of payment to Rebecca Young for making "Continental Standards." (She continues to make various items for military stores through 1782-3 and into 1786.)

March 3, 1782   Unbeknownst to Elizabeth Ashburn, her husband dies in a British prison.

May 5, 1782   Barton, working with the third committee, develops a design for the Great Seal which he describes as including "...thirteen stars disposed in a circle representing a new Constellation, which alludes to the new Empire, formed in the World by the Confederation of those States ..."

July 2, 1782	An estimate for procuring "100 standards for the army, silk, the name of the state and the number of the Regiment to be done in a garter of blue with pure gold leaf" is reported by Samuel Hodgdon, CGMS. The records indicate that the number ordered was reduced to 50 (Richardson, page 263).
July 20, 1782	The final design of the Great Seal of the United States by Charles Thomson, after the design submitted by the Third Committee is rejected, is adopted by Congress (Patterson and Dougal).
March 10, 1783	From Headquarters, Washington writes to Colonel Timothy Pickering, "Sir: In Answer to a letter written by the Comr in Chief a week or two ago (several havg been written before on same subject) to the Secty of War, respectg the Standards for the Army. The following reply has been made. 'The Standards are in the Hands of the Q Master at Camp, and have been there fore some time.' The Commander in Chief requests your Explanation of the Matter." Pickering answered the same day (March 10) that the standards came to the store at camp in a box with other articles. The field commissary of military stores removed the other articles, "but left the standards, saying he would send for them; however, there they are yet set."
March 11, 1783	From Headquarters, Washington writes to Secretary of War, "Sir: I am honored with your several letters of 26th Feby, 1st, and 4th of March. ...The Standards, I have found, by examining, to be in the care of Mr. Frothingham, F.C. of Military Stores. Your Intimation in your last, was the first Notice, I had, of them being near me."
May 8, 1783	Elizabeth Ashburn marries John Claypoole (who had brought her the news of her previous husband's death).
1783	The Free Quakers build their Meeting House (which is still standing) at Fifth and Arch.

1785	John and Elizabeth Claypoole become members of the Free Quakers.
1787	Hopkinson, while Judge of Admiralty, is Editor of the Columbian Magazine which publishes an engraving by James Trenchard of a ship flying an American ensign, with dots (stars) in three linear rows. (Moeller, NAVA News, 35/1)
1790	Hopkinson is appointed Judge of the United States Court of the Eastern District of Pennsylvania by Washington.
May 9, 1791	Hopkinson dies suddenly of apoplexy.
1791	Philadelphia Directory of Clement Biddle lists Betsy's third husband John Claypoole, upholsterer, at 80 South Second Street. At that time, John had a position with the Custom House, so this listing can be construed as representing the family business in the husband's name. (Timmins and Yarrington, 1983)
1794	Congress alters the "Naval" flag of the United States by voting to add two additional stars and two additional stripes representing two additional states that have joined the Union. The stars are configured in five rows of three. In voting for the new flag, a motion to designate it as the "Established flag of the United States" (to avoid the necessity of making later changes) is defeated in favor of the motion to designate it as the "Flag of the United States."
1785—forward	Richardson (1982) notes that "For 50 or more years following the Revolution, the flag with an eagle and stars was a popular alternative to the stars and stripes." The flag carried by the army in 1787 was a blue flag with an eagle and eight-pointed stars filling the center of the flag, no stripes. In 1812 there were seventeen red and white stripes on the eagle's breast, and seventeen stars above and around the eagle. The stars are five-pointed. This flag is carried until 1834. (Thruston)

1810, 1811, and 1816
      Elizabeth Claypoole is engaged in making flags for the Indian Department.

August 1813
      In Baltimore, Mary Pickersgill (daughter of Rebecca Young) makes the "Star Spangled Banner" which flew over Fort McHenry. She is given this job because of family connections with Commodore Barney and General Stricker. (Purdy letter)

1827
      Betsy moves to the home of married daughter Susan Satterthwaite in the remote suburb of Abington near Philadelphia. (Thompson 1972)

1830
      Philadelphia City Directory of the 1830s lists "Elizabeth Claypoole, Upholsterer, 74 South Front Street." Ray Thompson (1972) states that Betsy gave up active work on the business in 1827 so the 1830 listing may represent the ongoing family business.

January 30, 1836
      Elizabeth Claypoole dies in the home of her daughter Jane Canby in Philadelphia.

1851
      A painting by Ellie Wheeler of Philadelphia, daughter of famed artist Thomas Sully, depicts Betsy Ross showing three men a flag with the stars in a circle. The painting eerily presages the Weisgerber painting of 1893, and was done 19 years before William Canby brought the Betsy Ross story to the attention of the American public. It suggests that her role in making our earliest flag was commonly accepted in early Philadelphia.

1852
      Captain Schuyler Hamilton asserts that the first American Flag was a Stars and Stripes with the stars in a circle, noting that many variations existed.

1852
      The famous painting of Washington Crossing the Delaware by Emanuel Leutze features the "New Constellation" flag, reflecting the symbolic nature of that flag design.

1870   Wm. J. Canby gives a speech on Betsy Ross, his grandmother, to the Historical Society of Pennsylvania.

1887   Major General Schuyler Hamilton (retired) now recognizes that the 3-2-3-2-3 variation of the arrangement of the stars in the canton was very popular, he says, because the stars fell along the lines of the crosses in the old British flag, and the soldiers and sailors readily identified with it.

1893   Charles H. Weisgerber does the painting of Betsy, with the flag with stars in a circle on her lap and the three men in the room, that becomes the centerpiece of the Certificate of Membership sold to patriotic citizens for 10 cents to raise money to purchase the Flag House, Betsy's former home in Philadelphia.

June 12, 1992   Wall Street Journal featured article on Betsy Ross triggers research and discovery of corroborating evidence to support the family story.

Genealogy

Family Line of John Balderston Harker

Elizabeth Griscom, commonly known as BETSY ROSS
Married (1) John Ross, ~~4/11/1773~~, no children *11/4/73*
Married (2) Joseph Ashburn, 6/15/1777, two children with one surviving child
    Aucilla (Zilla) b. 9/15/1779, died young
    Eliza Ashburn, b. 2-25-1781, married Captain Isaac Silliman (no further information)
Married (3) **John Claypoole**, 5/8/17~~8~~, five children with four surviving children
    Clarissa Sidney, b. 4-3-1785, married Jacob Wilson, 6/4/1805, d 7-10-1864
    Susan, b. 11/15/1786, married Abel Satterthwaite 11/12/1812,
    Rachel, b. 2/1/1789, married 1st Edward Jones, 2nd John Fletcher, 4/10/1823
    Jane, b. 11/13/1792, married Caleb Canby, 7/2/1818, d 1/4/1873
    Harriet, b. 12/20/1795, died age 9 months.

Jane Claypoole/ Caleb Canby, married 7/2/1818
    Catherine, b 5/16/1819, married Lloyd Balderston, 11/9/1843, d 2/10/1884
    Elizabeth, b. 10/10/1820, unmarried
    Charles, b. 8/6/1822, married Susan Kirk, d 6/17/1851
    John, b. 10/8/1823, married Elizabeth Bowster
    William, b. 8/1/1825, married Caroline Prescott, d 1/10/1890
        (William GAVE THE SPEECH to the HISTORICAL SOCIETY of
        PENNSYLVANIA in 1870)
    Caleb, b. ? , married Mary Prestwick, d 12/10/1859
    George, b. 3/13/1829, married Matilda Goodwin
        (George RESEARCHED the HISTORY and WROTE the BOOK after
        William's death)
    Jane, b. 3/8/1831, married Abel J. Hopkins, d 4/30/1881
    Mary, b. 4/20/1833, married Robert S. Culin

Catherine Canby/Lloyd Balderston married 11/9/1843

    Annie, b. 9/7/1844, unmarried

    George, b. 6/23/1846, married Myra Atwater, (sister to Sarah below)

    Canby, b. 8/24/1847, married Mary Anne Brown

    John, b. 2/22/1849, married Anna E. Marshall

    Jane, b. 1/16/1851, married Samuel Morris Jones

    Charles, b. 3/17/1852, married Effie V. Dillaye

    Catherine, b. 5/14/1854, died young, 7/3/1858

    William, b. 8/30/1856, married Stella Seime

    Elwood, b. 6/9/1858, married Sarah Atwater, (sister to **Myra** above)

    Mark, b. 5/30/1860

    Alice, b. 9/20/1861, died young, 12/5/1864

    Lloyd, b. 7/3/1863, married Mary F. Alsop

        (Lloyd PUBLISHED the research and writing of George Canby
        "The Evolution of the American Flag" 1909)

George Balderston/Myra Atwater, married 12/1878

    Mary A. b. 10/16/1879

    Edward, b. 3/21/1881

    Alice, b. 11/22/1882

    Catherine, b. 8/9/1884, died young 5/9/1886

    Jane Canby, b. 4/21/1886

    Bertha, b. 1/4/1888

    Anne, b. 9/11/1889

    Levi, b. 5/8/1891

    Sarah, b. 9/26/1892, married Herbert Harker (Jr.)

    Ruth, b. 2/7/1895

Sarah Balderston/Herbert Harker (Jr.), married 2/6/1915

    William, b. 1/20/1916

    George, b. 10/2/1918

    John, b. 6/21/22, married Isabella Roberts, 5/20/1944

    Kate, b. 11/5/1924

About the Author

John Balderston Harker, fifth generation descendent of Betsy Ross, was born on June 21st, 1922 in Milwaukee, Wisconsin. His family moved to Cleveland, Ohio and in the third grade, the class held a skit on the making of the first American flag. John played the part of George Washington coming to meet Betsy Ross and have her make a flag for him. It was then that his family told him of the legend and connection to Betsy.

His family moved to Cheltenham, Pennsylvania when he was twelve. He graduated from Cheltenham High School in 1940 where he met his lovely wife, Isabella, with whom he has been happily married for 60 plus years. He received his B.A. in Liberal Arts from Temple University and his M.A. in Psychology from the University of Pennsylvania in 1949. He had a distinguished career helping the banking industry improve employee relations with the introduction of structured salary administration, personnel assessments and attitude surveys. His work helped better the working environment for employees and managers of banks throughout the Northeast and elsewhere.

John's family was Quaker, but as a practical matter he was active in the Methodist Church in his youth. Once married, living in Massachusetts, and running his own consulting business, The Harker Organization Inc, John, Isabella and their four children became Unitarian Universalists. John and Isabella were always involved with social concerns. John always stayed in touch with his Quaker relatives, many times on trips attending meeting with the Balderston clan down in Colora, Maryland. When the family moved to Falmouth, Massachusetts in 1983, John and Isabella returned to being practicing Quakers as members of Sandwich Monthly Meeting. They attend Space Coast Friends Meeting during their winter stays in Florida.

After retirement, and with a passion for family history, John became aware of the negative views of historians towards the story attributed to his ancestor Betsy Ross. He was concerned that what he had always believed to be a family truth was being questioned, and even denied any validity whatsoever. Therefore, he set out to ascertain the facts for himself.

For several years in Falmouth, he acquainted himself with all the information available on the flag, and continued his research when they moved to Florida to be in a warmer climate. Summering on Cape Cod and wintering in Florida, and always engaged in following up on leads to uncover new information, John slowly unearthed more and more family history. He found numerous resources that helped him uncover previously unknown facts to bolster the family story. In the adventure and search for Truth, he has learned that the Truth can be elusive, and that history is not an exact science.

Permissions

All exhibits, images, art, and graphics used with permission, as follows:

Front plate from copper stamp, date unkown, digital postive & negative. Courtesy of owner.

The *Portrait of Betsy Ross* by Samuel L. Waldo. Courtesy of the owner.

Betsy Ross five-pointed Pattern for Stars. Courtesy of the Society of Free Quakers.

Birth of Our Nation's Flag, 1893, by Charles H. Weisgerber. Courtesy Charles H. Weisgerber II.

Betsy Ross and the Flag Committee by Ellie (Sully) Wheeler, 1851. Courtesy of Weston Adams.

The Making of Our Flag by J. L. G. Ferris (c. 1900-1910). Used with permission of the owner.

George Washington at Princeton, by Charles Willson Peale, (1779). Used with permission from the Pennsylvania Academy of Fine Arts.

George Washington (1732-1799) at the Battle of Princeton, Jan. 3, 1777, Princeton University. Used with permission from Princeton University.

Bucks of America Regimental Flag. Used with permission from the Massachusetts Historical Society, Boston, MA, Bridgeman Art Library.

Proposed Frescoes, Ladies Waiting Room, (1856). Courtesy Architect of the Capital, Washington, D.C.

Hopkinson's proposed design of the Great Seal; Charles Thomson's design of June 29, 1782; *Great Seal of the United States* as adopted by Congress in 1782; and Robert Trenchard's engraving in 1786 representative of the Great Seal. Courtesy of the American Philosophical Society, Philadelphia, Pa.

Ledger Page, (1812) Society of Free Quakers, *Excerpts from the Minutes of Meeting for Business, Society of Free Quakers,* (1847), and January 6th, 1847, *Minute of meeting of the Free Quaker Dorcas Society.* Courtesy of the American Philosophical Society, Philadelphia, Pennsylvania.

Betsy Ross House, circa 1876, with portrait of Elizabeth Claypoole in window. Courtesy, Betsy Ross House/Historic Philadelphia, Inc. Copyright 2003.

Certificate of Membership, American Flag House and Betsy Ross Memorial Association, issued 1905. Courtesy of the owner.

Richardson, Edward W. *Standards and Colors of the American Revolution*, Philadelphia: University of Pennsylvania Press and Pennsylvania Society of Sons of the Revolution, 1982.

Roberts, Cokie. *Founding Mothers*, New York: Harper Collins Publishers Inc. , 2004.

Schermerhorn, Frank Earle. *American and French Flags of the Revolution, 1775-1783*. Philadelphia: Pennsylvania Society of Sons of the Revolution, 1948.

Sellers, Charles Coleman. *Charles Willson Peale*. New York: Scribner's, 1969.

Sizer, Theodore. *The Works of Colonel John Trumbull, Artist of the American Revolution*. New Haven: Yale University Press, 1967.

Smith, Whitney. *The Flag Book of the United States*. New York: William Morrow and Company, Inc., 1970.

_____. *Face to Face with Betsy Ross*. The Flag Bulletin, vol. 14, no. 1 (January-February 1975).

Smolinski, Diane. *Important People of the Revolutionary War*. Chicago: Reed Educational and Professional Publishing, 2002.

Society of Free Quakers. Papers. American Philosophical Society, Philadelphia.

Spargo, John. *The Stars and Stripes in 1777: An Account of the Birth of the Flag and Its First Baptism of Fire*. Bennington, VT: Bennington Battle Monument and Historical Association, 1928.

Thompson, Ray. *Betsy Ross, Last of Philadelphia's Free Quakers*. Fort Washington, PA: The Bicentennial Press, 1972.

Thruston, R.C. Ballard. *The Origin and Evolution of the United States Flag*. Washington, D.C.: GPO, 1926. U.S. House. 69th Cong., 1st sess., 1926. H. Doc. 258.

Timmins, Dr. William D. and Robert W. Yarrington, Jr. *Betsy Ross: The Griscom Legacy*. Salem County, NJ: Cultural and Heritage Commission through the auspices of the Salem County Board of Chosen Freeholders, 1983.

United States Department of State. *The Great Seal of the United States. Bureau of Public Affairs. Office of Public Communications, Washington, D.C.* Publication No. 10411, September 1996.

Walker, Anthony. *So Few the Brave: Rhode Island Continentals, 1775-1783.* Newport, RI: Seafield Press, 1981.

Wetherill, Charles. *History of the Religious Society of Friends Called by Some the Free Quakers in the City of Philadelphia.* Washington, D.C.: Ross & Perry, Inc. 1894.

Zall, Paul M. *Comical Spirit of Seventy-Six: The Humor of Francis Hopkinson.* San Marino, CA: Huntington Library, 1976.

INDEX

Q

Quaife, Milo 77
Quaker, Committee of Women Friends 29
Quaker, Orthodox 32
Quaker, Society of 33, 103
Quaker Meeting House, Free 35
Quakers, Society of Free 6, 28, 32-36, 51, 59, 89, 92, 99, 106
Quilt, Sherman 67

R

Ranger 76
Read, George 42
Read, William 30
Regiment of Black Soldiers 18
Reid, Captain Samuel Chester 97
Rhode Island Regiment 81, 113
Richards, Captain William 7, 9, 41
Roberts, Cokie 65
Rodney, Daniel 92
Ross, Colonel George 2, 5, 22, 29, 37-39, 41-42, 51-52, 60-62, 105
Ross, William 2, 19
Rush, Dr. Benjamin 47, 68-69, 124
Rush, Richard 68-69

S

Sampson, Deborah 45
Say, Dr. Benjamin 32
Schuyler, General Philip 3
Scott, Robert 84
Seal, Engraving of the Great 84
Secret Committee 4, 52

Seller, Susan 46, 51, 63, 120
Serapis 16
Sheaff, Richard 80
Sherman, Rebecca Prescott 40, 65-67, 69, 94
Sherman, Roger 40, 65-66
Skillman, Helen 80
Smith, Dr. Whitney 43-44, 56, 80-81
Smithsonian Institute 42
Snyder County Historical Society, The 126, 128
Society of Free Quakers 6, 28, 34-36, 51, 59, 89, 92, 99, 106
Sousa, John Philip 20
Spanish-American War 20
St. Leger, Brigadier General Barry 57
Star of English Heraldry 63
Stark, General John 87
Stars, European heraldic six-pointed 88
Stars Artifact 89, 94, 99
Stevens, B. F. 56
Sully, Thomas 41
Summers, Mark 96

T

Talmadges's Dragoons of Connecticut 17
Testimonies 40, 59-60, 62-64, 94, 118
Thompson, Ray 6, 28
Thomson, Charles 53, 84
Timmins, Dr. 89, 91
Trenchard, Robert 84

V

Valley Forge 45, 57, 114
Van Ness Throop, John Peter 84